I0122726

AFTER THE STORM

A True Story of Tragedy, Survival, and Hope

DR. LAUREN FARMER

LANDON
HAIL
PRESS

Copyright© 2023 Lauren Farmer
All Rights Reserved

Paperback ISBN: 978-1-959955-02-3
Hardback ISBN: 978-1-959955-15-3
Cover design by Caitlyn Hampton
Published by Landon Hail Press

Scripture from the Holy Bible, New International Version®, NIV®. Copyright ©
1973, 1978, 1984, 2011 by Biblica, Inc.® Used by permission. All rights
reserved worldwide.
Scripture from the Holy Bible, New Living Translation. Copyright © 1996, 2004,
2007 by Tyndale House Foundation. Used by permission of Tyndale House
Publishers, Inc., Carol Stream, Illinois 60188. All rights reserved.
Scripture personal paraphrase from The Living Bible by Kenneth N. Taylor. First
copyright, 1971 by Tyndale House Publishers. Used by permission of
Tyndale House Publishers, Inc., Carol Stream, Illinois 60188. All rights
reserved.
Scripture from the Holy Bible, International Children's Bible®. Copyright© 1986,
1988, 1999, 2015 by Thomas Nelson. Used by permission. All rights
reserved.
Scripture from the Holy Bible, the Passion Translation. Copyright 5-Fold Media
2017 Used by permission of BroadStreet® Publishing, Savage, MN. All Rights
Reserved.
Verses taken from The Message, Copyright © by Eugene H. Peterson 1993, 1994,
1995, 1996, 2000, 2001, 2002. Used by permission of NavPress Publishing
Group.
Additional verses quoted from the Catholic Public Domain Version (CPDV),
2009.

DISCLAIMER: Although the author and publisher have made every effort to ensure the
accuracy and completeness of information contained in this book, we assume no
responsibility for errors, inaccuracies, omissions, or any inconsistency herein. Any slights on
people, places, or organizations are unintentional. The material in this book is provided for
educational purposes only. Some details may have been changed to protect the privacy of
those involved.

I dedicate this book first and foremost to my husband. Your support, love, and strength have helped me get through the hardest of times. You are God's gift to my life, and I know He moved mountains to make sure our paths crossed and everything aligned so that two crazy, stubborn people would fall in love, start a family, and complete His mission for us.

After eight years, we are still early on in this journey together, and I'm so thankful we get to keep doing life together. If we can make it through building two houses, a pandemic, surviving a natural disaster, and blending our two lives in order to raise a family, we can do anything. And that's exciting. I will probably still lose my temper when I tell you to look in the fridge *again* for some item you just can't seem to find, and you will probably roll your eyes if I come home from Homegoods one more time with another thing "we just had to have," which we always end up using, but that's okay. You'll be there to tell me when it's time to get in our storm shelter if bad weather comes, and I'll be here trying new recipes and giving you some new home improvement project or gardening task. We just work, and I just love you.

Secondly, I want to dedicate this book to the Cookeville community. Without this town, Kory and I would be long gone, trying to pick up the broken pieces and rebuild our lives from afar. Instead, you created a place that's been welcoming, loving, and has helped us in so many ways. You helped us pick up our belongings and clear our lot. Financially, you helped relieve some pressure, too. But most of all, you showed us love and friendship at every corner.

I wrote this book to help you heal in places you may not know you needed healing and to help people going through storms of their own. We can all get through this, but it's easier when we do it together.

CONTENTS

FOREWORD

Box upon box and truckload after truckload, Lauren continued to coordinate with the sheriff's department to distribute supplies to those who needed them. A semi-truck-load of donations and a drive-through pickup line is where I saw Lauren find her calling after the storm.

We were told about a large truckload of donations that was sitting in the sheriff's department parking lot for survivors of the tornado. Not having anything to truly call our own, we decided to go check it out.

After signing our names and sharing a bit of our story with the men in charge of the donations, Lauren caught a glimpse of diapers, baby formula, and an assortment of baby clothes. It was at that moment that I knew we would be busy. I could see the determination in her eyes to empty this entire eighteen-wheeler and get these supplies to those who needed them.

Lauren coordinated with the sheriff's department for the next few weeks, to connect individuals who were in need after the tornado and distribute these donations. The sheriff's department was having difficulty getting individuals to come to the parking lot where the donations were set up for distribution, but Lauren knew she could connect with those affected by the tornado. She shared her story with them while she discovered their needs and fulfilled them with the help of the sheriff's department.

She didn't feel the need to receive these gifts herself; she was more concerned with those she felt needed them more than she did, despite having lost everything.

That is my wife. That is the mother of my boys. That is the Christian woman who emerged after the storm.

First of all, what the hell is a foreword and who even reads it? Anytime I read a book, I always skip the front-of-the-book stuff and jump straight into Chapter 1.

Hello, I'm Kory, and I am lucky enough to have married the author of this book. All jokes aside, when she asked me to write this, I felt nervous, like I was back in school and looking to make a certain grade. I wasn't sure if I would find the right words to describe my wife in a way that would do her justice so that you could get an inside look at the woman I see.

Kind Hearted. Loving. Caring. Faithful. These are the words I chose to describe my wife.

We met in St. Augustine more than ten years ago, on my birthday and by fate. We didn't really get along at first, because she was too controlling and uptight to relax, and I was too stubborn to back down. But she was beautiful, a firecracker, and had a heart of gold. After spending more and more time together, we both let down our walls and finally saw each other for our true selves: a Southern gentleman from Tennessee and a smart, high-achieving Florida girl whose paths were meant to cross.

After we got married, we settled into life together in my home state. It meant a lot to me that she was willing to leave her security and family to join me in Tennessee, where I would be her husband and protector and we would start over together. I was grateful she was willing to work those long hours while I was able to study and work part-time, and yet, we still made time for those home-cooked meals I married her for. We strived to make our apartment a home and to build our friend group during our busy season. She was supportive of my schooling and even prepared dinner for me and my classmates after our long study sessions.

Before the storm, Lauren was overly concerned with what people thought of her and was a habitual people-pleaser. Her actions were led by expectations and a desire to achieve. Afterward, she morphed into a confident woman, secure in her religion, who didn't care what people thought, because she knew what her purpose was. She had always tried to help others, but now she didn't let anything stand in her way.

Not only did she gain strength, but the tornado also broke her. I watched her lose everything she ever had, and then, for a while, she could no longer give to those around her and had to receive. This changed her for the best, because she learned to appreciate the help she always wanted to give. She no longer had anything to prove to anyone, but knew that her worth stood in God. We were saved from death that night to fulfill higher purposes, and I could tell that she found hers.

As she wrote this book, I didn't want to read it for a while. It was hard to relive the hard moments, but once I did read it, I realized there were a lot of happy moments I'd forgotten about, too. To summarize what we've been able to overcome and achieve since that night was quite a task, and I'm not surprised at all that she was able to complete this book. She wrote this book as a mother of a one-year-old, working full time, being pregnant, running a business, and putting up with me and two dogs. I knew she could write the book when she first told me about the idea three years ago, but now that she's finished it, I'm very proud of her for achieving her goal.

I know this book has the potential to help so many people overcome tragedy, loss, or hard times. I pray that this book is successful, but not for us. For others' lives to be touched, and so they understand that no matter what happens in their lives, no matter what hell they live through, they will always be able to find comfort in God.

Sweet Pea, I love you so much and am very proud of you.

Love,

Kory Farmer, BSN, RN
Proud husband, father of Beau, Theo, Shadow, and Xena, and Go Vols!

PROLOGUE

"Are you okay?!" Kory asked me after the world stopped moving around us. I wasn't sure if he was yelling, whispering, or gasping. I felt nothing and everything all at once. Numb, perhaps. I had no idea which way was up and which way was down.

I grasped a handful of a dog's coat in my left hand, held an empty dog collar in the right, and lay down on top of what might have been pillows, with Kory semi on top of me and semi by my side.

"I... I don't know."

I didn't think I was hurt, but I had no idea what had happened.

Kory pushed what felt like a wall off of us, and I tried to sit up. I felt my phone by my side, and then, all of a sudden, it was bright. I had been able to see just fine before he found the lantern, but now it was clearly bright. It was also deathly quiet, which was an odd contrast compared to the train that had just run us over.

But just as that thought crossed my mind, the screams started.

INTRODUCTION

Do you ever wonder how in the world you've survived something? Whether it's a life-altering tornado that kills your neighbors and leaves destruction where a beautiful home used to stand, or a series of unfortunate events that continue to wear you down until you feel like you have no more to give, it's meant to kill our faith, our sanity, and disrupt our daily lives. How in the world do we know we are going to be okay and that we are not alone?

Have you ever stopped to think back to all of the ways you've made it through because of how you've been prepared for this exact moment? Whether or not you realize it, we have been tested, prepped, and given plenty of defenses to help us navigate this oh-so-imperfect world.

If you had told me these things three years ago, I would have thought you were crazy. I would have told you, "Life is a series of coincidences" and you "get what you get," regardless of how it makes you feel.

Sure, I was religious. I believed in Jesus and went to church events when they fit into my schedule. I did the church thing when it was convenient for me. I went through the motions to be a good person and go out of my way to help people, but I attributed this to my solid upbringing and a caring Southern heart.

I knew I was meant for great things, but that could have meant greatness in my physical therapy career. It could have meant greatness in the children I would raise or the money I would donate. I didn't have what I thought was significant trauma in my past; I didn't have crazy unrealistic expectations for my future. My excellent but simple life seemed pretty ordinary and pretty boring. I had no idea that throughout what I perceived to be my fun, but relatively safe life, events would occur that were preparing me for more.

You see, God knows what we need before we even know we need it, and before we can ask for it, He's already made it a reality. I want to share how I survived one of the most traumatic events in my town's history because of the preparation God made in my life. I want to share how He used this tragedy to create my story to share with you and to touch the lives of people who think their story may be a little ordinary, too, or who maybe don't know just what their life is all about. The best part of that is, we don't have to create our story; we just have to live our lives, making the best decisions we can, one day at a time.

A word of advice to the wise: don't let God know you think you're ordinary, because that's when extraordinary things are right around the corner.

CHAPTER 1

Just Be Yourself

Romans 5:8: "But God demonstrates His own love for us in this: While we were still sinners Christ died for us."

I wasn't raised in the church. I wasn't super-religious and didn't understand God. Despite all of this, He still loved me. I was a different person before the tornado, figuring out who I wanted to be and how I would make my mark on the world, and I made a lot of mistakes and was taught a lot of lessons in my journeys. I was wronged and hurt, and I put up walls many times throughout my life, but throughout all of the struggles, I was still able to grow through all those barriers to become the person God made me ultimately to be.

The journey to find ourselves and our place in the world is just that: a journey. It's not a destination we reach or a moment we come to. It's not something we finally achieve and then can quit trying to reach. This is something I didn't understand at first, because, when you're young, your goals have markers for when you reach them. Win a competition, goal met. Get straight As for a school year, goal met. Don't get grounded for the summer, goal partially met.

It wasn't until after college that I really started to understand that just because you're an adult doesn't mean you have it all together. When I became a mom, I realized I have it even less together than I'd originally thought.

Life doesn't get easier, and tasks don't become less stressful. Rather, we become more resilient and learn that we need to give grace just as much as we need to ask for it. We figure out that everyone, ourselves included, is just trying to do the best dang job we can do.

Writing this down makes me realize that all the instances when I may have been wronged or misled when I was younger were not necessarily because some adult or other person intended to harm me; it was because they are not all-knowing and all-seeing and are just as imperfect as I am.

As a young child, before we are inundated with the social expectations and learned hierarchy of the world and the people in it, we all just exist. There are relationships on different levels, of course. You have your mom and dad, any siblings or cousins, friends, relatives, and acquaintances. You may develop preferences, such as only letting Mom hug you, or preferring not to play with a mean friend, but the thought of popularity is not an innate thing we consider. That is, we don't consider it until we are taught about it.

This usually happens during our first years of school, when children begin making choices about who to hang out with on the playground or whether someone gets pointed out or laughed at for behavior, rejecting or casting them aside. We become aware of actions, characteristics, and relationships that cause others to not necessarily like or dislike you, but to see favor or not in you. These social constructs are generally built on social expectations found in the society we grow up in.

My first encounter with the popularity game began when we moved from a small island off the mainland of Japan, where my dad had been stationed for over four years, to north Florida, or the

Redneck Riviera, as my mother likes to call it. As I entered the fourth grade, I was the new girl; I hadn't grown up with these people who had all known one another their whole lives and been in school together since kindergarten. I had gone from one set of social expectations and standards in my advanced classes in Japan to a completely different one in the States, and I realized for the first time that I was different.

Previously, half of my schooling had been in Japanese, and before I'd left, we had just begun to learn the art of symbol drawing for the characters of the Japanese Kanji alphabet. It involved intricate brush strokes and was an art in itself, creating phrases and meaning out of the characters drawn. I knew enough Japanese to carry on a conversation, and I could read children's books in the language almost as well as I could read them in English. Fun fact, Japanese is written top to bottom and right to left!

When people found out that this abnormally small, blonde girl had these hidden talents, it intrigued them. Then they would ask questions and bring attention to my abilities, leading others to also find out I was different. As an outsider, all I wanted to do was to fit in and be the same as all my other classmates, but with this attention, I couldn't do that. I began to shy away, pretend not to remember, and spend my own time coloring and drawing after finishing school work.

Then, as teachers noticed my boredom increase, halfway through the school year I was placed in an advanced classroom and had to, yet again, adapt to a new environment, new classmates, and new people who would know I was different. Needless to say, I didn't fit in very well and did my best to be invisible.

I was too small to be picked anything but last for kickball at recess, and I was too new to be known by all the kids in school. A little more than a year later, it was middle-school time. By then, I had become heavily involved in gymnastics, and all my after-school time was spent at the gym or with my teammates, further dividing me from schoolmates. This continued on into high school, and let's just say, being popular was never something I was able to master or really even understand.

Before my senior year, I decided I would attempt to boost my social standing, and so I tried out for cheerleading, mostly just to prove I could make it without experience. Although I made the team, that's about all I could say about that experience.

You see, I viewed cheerleading as another sport, just as gymnastics and swim team had been. We practiced, knew routines, ran and did sit ups, tumbled and stunted. Football games, to me, were just the way we showed off our skills and everything we had worked for. So, when it was time for our first game, I showed up in uniform, with pompoms in my bag and a choker bandana around my neck like all the others, but I had to learn a very important lesson that day. Cheerleading was definitely about showing off, but it wasn't just our athleticism we were parading.

Oh no. I showed up with a messy bun—who knew "hair up" meant in a manicured ponytail with a ribbon? I wore zero makeup— why would I waste the time wearing makeup when I would just be tumbling and sweating anyway? And I got my ankles wrapped with the football players, due to my old gymnastics' injuries, so I could tumble on the field. I hardly knew the cheers, and I vividly recall a very gracious younger teammate mouthing the lyrics to cheers as they were called, trying to inconspicuously show me the movements before we began them in sync. I was a hot mess at this flashy side to the sport I thought I had joined.

I was not good at those parts. I could tumble, I could dance, and I loved stunting, even though I wasn't given much chance to try it out, but cheering and remembering which words to shout when—

I could not. Especially not with a smile on my face and a tilt of my head in the right direction.

I was so far removed from that social group that I didn't understand the gravity of the situation when two girls got kicked off the squad for drinking before a game, even though I had seen them hanging out in a Jeep with locked doors, passing something back and forth. All of these misunderstandings and my inability to follow, or care to follow, social cues always led to difficulties fitting in plus an overall poor rating on the general popularity scale. I mean, I couldn't even get nominated to homecoming court for the math team during my senior year, despite my recent "cheerleader" title! The math team was something I had even been a part of for seven years.

Things didn't change much when I went to college. I was seventeen and taking a full load of engineering classes with male-dominated subjects. Heck, even when I decided to join a sorority my sophomore year, my group of friends and I were the last to be invited to parties, never invited to be on welcoming committees, and, because of our differences, we definitely lacked the general popular vote. We all marched to the beat of our own drums, participating only in events we wanted to, balking at the general social constructs, and prioritizing our own desires over the good of the house.

Graduate school continued along the same pattern. Even when I became the student body president and a class representative, I knew that any favor I had redounded from my boyfriend (now husband) and the tolerance of his friends.

It wasn't until adulthood, when I moved to a different city, established myself as a professional, and found my own friends instead of friends of convenience and fellow students, that I truly found peace with my friend circle and social circumstances. For the first time in my life, there was nothing I felt I had to prove to anyone else. If I didn't fit in, that was okay; we didn't hang out. If we didn't have common interests, that was okay; other people did. There was no more obligation, no more expectation, and, overall, this led to fewer insecurities. I was who I was, and I was becoming okay with that.

Why, then, was popularity such a struggle for me as a child and early adult? I've pondered and pondered this, because I don't want my children to go through feeling ostracized and outcast, like I had felt. The conclusion I have come to not only lies in my own insecurities and general opposition to the general consensus, but in other people's insecurities and need to fit in, too. You see, growing up, if I didn't want to do something, I usually didn't do it. I didn't want to join the band, so I didn't. I wanted to pursue math and join the math team, so I did. I wanted to prove I could be a cheerleader without experience, so I tried out, worked for it, and did it. I didn't want to drink and party, so I didn't.

Sometimes, I think, as insecure people, teenagers especially, we desire to fit in so badly that we convince ourselves we want what everyone else says *they* want, just so we can be seen as cool or accepted. We don't want to be the outsider, whether that looks like: a superb piano player, a math whiz, an elite athlete, fluent in many languages, or any other hidden talents we have that separate us from the general crowd.

Many people sacrifice themselves and whom they want to be for this drive to fit in. This may mean downplaying their abilities or desires, denying religion, graying the lines of their morals, or just yearning so much for a friend that they will literally do whatever it takes. I think it's why we see so many people who always feel like outcasts from society and why some of their peers turn to acting out. By denying yourself and your abilities, you lose who you want to be in exchange for fitting in, until you get so far down that rabbit hole, you don't have a clue what your dreams or desires are anymore. You just need to feel seen.

The funny thing is, moving to a new town in which I could choose whom I hung out with and what I did with my time allowed me to center myself with like-minded people. Becoming comfortable in my own skin and learning that other people liked me for being me bolstered my confidence and grew my desire to want to like others for whom they were, too. It built my confidence to stand by my beliefs and morals, so when I felt that a job asked me to go beyond my boundaries, I could leave and pursue my career elsewhere. It meant, when others drank at a party and wanted to keep partying elsewhere and I was tired, I could go home. When you become confident in doing what you want to do, there are no longer any outside standards to meet and expectations to live up to. You just get to be you. And if you hang out with the right people who accept that about you, they begin to embrace that in themselves, as well.

How do we teach this "be yourself" attitude to our children, who so obviously struggle with identity and fitting in? How do we tell younger and less experienced people that if you truly are yourself and pursue what you want, the popularity and social favor will come? People are drawn to confidence and sure-footedness, so I believe it starts with helping people be confident in who they really are. The more we try to be like everyone else, the easier we lose diversity, creativity, and the growth society requires to thrive.

Recently, I went to a personal development conference, where they played a video that has stood out in my mind ever since. It was a bunch of people lounging in a field, perhaps at some music festival. Then, one guy decided he was bored or ready for something new, so he stood up and started to dance.

This was not just a step-clap sequence; it was a full-on self-moshing rager with circular movements. It included arm-flailing and a twisting around that garnered a lot of outside attention. At first, others just stared and laughed to themselves and their friends, thinking how ridiculous he looked. However, the young man carried on, clearly enjoying himself.

After a while, someone else said to themselves, "What the heck!" And they joined right in. That led to another person and another, until the whole crowd was moving and dancing about together. There was no music, but everyone was laughing and being goofy and not worrying about the person next to them or what they may be thinking about their moves.

The first person to do something may look weird and out of place, initially, but when other people get over themselves and find the desire to join in, it can become a beautiful dance party, where nobody is judging anyone else and everyone is just having a good time. The lesson to be found here is that it's really hard to stand up and be the first person to do anything out of the ordinary, but sometimes that leads to a damn good time. It's hard to do something against popular opinion.

Something else I've learned over time is we are all usually too busy worrying about ourselves and what other people may think of us, so we don't have time to judge others and what they may be doing over there. If you take a moment to stop and look around, you'll find that nobody is really looking at you, because they are too busy worrying about the people who they think are looking at them. Imagine the anxiety we could all save if we just agreed that being ourselves and doing what we wanted was okay.

What if it was better than okay? As we step into our true selves, we find that it's preferred and easier to just be us. As we continue to grow, we begin to accept that others are different, too—and that's okay. Wouldn't it be great if we could save ourselves this heartache growing up and just embrace our differences?

Through lots of learning, loving God, and learning to love myself, I have grown into a woman of acceptance and grace, and usually, I need more grace than I give out. It is through my journey of heartache and difficulty that I've come out on the other side, full of hope and love. I love myself, faults included, and I work daily at loving those around me, their faults included.

I hope to inspire a spark inside of you that can lead you toward a step in the direction of self-love, loving others, serving your community, and realizing that growth is constant. The only way I've been able to work toward all of these things is through finding God's love. The first step was just asking Him to help make my heart a little softer. The good news is, I didn't have to rely on myself for this—what a relief.

CHAPTER 2

How Did I Even Get Here?

Ephesians 4:1: "I urge you to live a life worthy of the calling you have received. Be completely humble and gentle; be patient, bearing with one another in love."

Each of us has a story about how we ended up where we are. Sometimes, it's simple, and sometimes, it's not. Sometimes, it's one career forever, and sometimes, it's restarting later in life. Whatever you do, do it with love and while serving the Lord, and everything will align.

IT's funny how we are led to our careers and professions. The decisions we make and the influence other people have on us, it all leads us to where we are. No matter the choices we make, I believe that God leads us to where we are meant to be, even if it takes Him opening door after different door for us, as we ignore each and every one. Gosh, what a stinking relief! I can't even imagine the pressure I'd feel, and the pressure I used to feel, thinking I was actually in control and responsible for making the right decisions every time.

What do you want to be when you grow up? I've heard that question too many times to count, and I'm sure I've asked it more times than I'd like to admit. I say this not because it's a silly question, but because of the hidden meaning behind it and the expectation it brings, unknown to the asker or the answerer.

How in the world are we supposed to know, really, at any age, what we want to commit to for the rest of our lives? How can we even know all of the options out there? Without diligent exposure from parents, teachers, and mentors, children may only be aware of your typical professions, like doctor, teacher, veterinarian, firefighter etc. These are all valiant choices, but what about the engineer, small business owner, computer analyst, plumber, electrician, nanny, and stay-at-home mom?

I say all this because, the truth is, I had no idea what I wanted to do. I was good at almost anything I tried, not because of talent, but because of dedication, meeting set expectations, and the determination I had not to fail. After moving from Japan back to the States, I had been a shy child and mostly kept to myself during class, drawing and coloring for hours, as I always finished my work early. This led to quick placement into advanced classes from a young age. There, I was challenged again, not only by the teachers, but by the high caliber of students around me.

A few different experiences led me to the profession I've been practicing for almost a decade. One was academics.

I took my first college course at age thirteen, as I entered high school. This was just expected of me and my classmates, with whom I'd grown up through earlier school years, and we took dual-enrolled geometry and college algebra II as freshmen. This led to AP classes, college credits, and a total of forty-two total class credits I achieved by age seventeen. At this young age, I travelled nearly four hours away to begin studying at the most prestigious school in the state.

Back to our original question: "What do you want to be?" This was so overwhelming because my path had been set for me for so long. Sure, I got to pick whether I would complete the harder classes or not, but how would I not? It's what I had always done. Just like I had been on the math team for seven years. I wasn't the best student or on the "A team" for math competitions, but I was in the top-level classes and keeping up with the A-teamers, completing Calculus II by senior year. I was almost a straight-A student and passed almost every AP test I took.

What's a girl to do when she's smart, driven, capable, and has no freaking clue? Well, she listens to her Southern momma, of course!

My mother always meant well and wanted the best for me. She never had intentions of pressure or coercion; she merely wanted to help me make the best decision she could. With all options considered, this meant helping me pursue a career in engineering. I was excellent at math, good enough at science, able to study hard, and had proven myself around male classmates, making the same grades and sometimes better.

This didn't mean much to me, and I wasn't even entirely sure what an engineer did except take hard classes in college. So, along with it I went. I had an excellent start with my high school classes and previous study habits. What was going to get in my way?

Well, my first year, I was blessed with a long-distance boyfriend, minimal distractions, and an amazing dorm neighbor who was taking many of the same classes and motivated me to attend class, study hard, and get good grades, just like I had always done.

The next year brought me a heart-wrenching break-up and a summer as an "experienced college student" returning home to curfews and expectations, before returning to school as a sophomore who knew what to expect. Something I knew I wanted was more friends and more social involvement. For me, this meant the Greek Life.

A whole new world of parties, philanthropy, study buddies, and sports involvement emerged, and with it, I forgot the sciences, the continuous study patterns, and my drive for good grades. I found that I could make it as a solid B student, keep my full-ride scholarship, and just change my major. So, that I did. Five times.

Thank goodness for my surplus of credits arriving at college, because without them, I would have tacked on at least another year of studies. I ended up graduating with a degree in Business Management and some advanced accounting classes, because, numbers. I had dabbled in exercise science and accounting, bouncing back and forth in the business school, before deciding I wanted to be a manager. I wasn't sure who would hire an inexperienced person who had barely managed her own four years at university, but I knew I would be great at it. Whatever "it" meant.

That was, until nobody would hire me. The year I graduated, we also experienced an economic downturn, and even those with countless years of experience couldn't get hired for jobs. I couldn't get a job as a receptionist with my four-year degree, 100 word/minute typing speed, and uncanny ability to ace any standardized test I was presented with. This left me working numerous jobs, holding down three at one point, including a bank teller for my 8-4, gymnastics coach in the evenings, and a server working Friday evenings and double shifts all weekend. It was a cycle I couldn't sustain, and I quickly decided I needed more.

In the past, I had entertained a semester's worth of classes with the idea of applying to physical therapy school, because I had been a high-level athlete with a myriad of injuries of my own that required intervention and recovery. The thoughts didn't last long, though, and I hadn't stayed on that route for very long. However, after everything else failed me, it became more and more appealing to go back to school and escape the apparent failure I was facing. I enrolled in some local evening classes and online classes, to make up a few of the credits I was missing, and I took the dreaded GRE, acing it, of course.

All that was left was the application. As luck would have it, I chose a school that had a paper application and an interview, two things I knew would put me ahead of other applicants. I applied to one school with a "D" on my last semester's transcript, a killer GRE score, and an affability to charm anyone with my more-than-mature responses. I got in on the first try.

This wasn't just a feat; it was a miracle. Others in my cohort had applied to multiple schools for multiple years. It didn't mean they weren't as good as me; it just meant I had certain advantages. I got in, and I thought I was set. I was smart, athletic, and ready to make new friends.

Another experience that would lead me to choosing to apply to physical therapy school was my own experience with months in physical therapy for personal rehabilitation. If you're familiar with gymnastics and the necessary dedication it takes to excel, you're aware of the amount of practice it takes to get there. Not only does it take a ton of time, but you end up doing a lot of dangerous things.

Everyone watches women's gymnastics every four years in the Olympics, and we all see the flips and twists and impossible landings on the four-inch beam. We get to witness the perfect landings, straight legs, and pointed toes. The smiling faces, the beautiful dance moves, and the grace that can't be mimicked in any other sport. What you don't see are the falls, the drills, the conditioning, the stretching, and the backbreaking moves and never-ending hours of practice it takes to get to that level. Ask any gymnast out there, and they will tell you, it's not about *if* you get injured, but *when* you get injured as a gymnast.

In high school, I worked out twenty-six hours per week at my peak level. That meant four-hour practices every day after school and six hours on Saturdays. That meant not much time for sleep and recovery and, often times, lots of fatigue, pushing and pushing to get better and better, and hard work toward that perfect ten or the next level or the next big skill.

I remember one of my first injuries was at the end of a floor rotation. We were doing front flips into a round off, to connect multiple skills into one tumbling pass. I was new to the skill, learning the right timing. One time, I opened up too late, over-rotating, and upon my landing, I hyper-extended my knee so badly, I couldn't put weight on it to limp over to my coach.

It's not like this everywhere, but the culture of gymnastics is that of a mom who is a nurse (just ask my husband and his brother): get up and walk it off, you're okay! In football, it's called a stinger, and the concept is the same. You're in temporary pain, but you'll be okay shortly. We are inadvertently taught to push through and work through the hard and the pain.

As a child, it's difficult to know when it's okay to do this and when it's not okay. I definitely didn't understand the difference yet, and I tried to get up from the ground, but tears immediately stung my eyes, and the pain shot through my leg like it was on fire. I was told to walk it off and I'd be okay..., but this time, I knew I wasn't okay.

In the aftermath of this injury, I did not see a doctor, did not go to rehab, and did not sit out for long. Ibuprofen was a hot commodity to handle swelling, paired with ice and elevation, but leaving out most of the rest associated with the famous RICE concoction expected with acute injuries. Rest. Ice. Compress. Elevate.

The next injury I experienced was to my wrists. I was doing back handsprings on the balance beam (a back flip landing on your hands before landing again on your feet), and my hands over-crossed, bending my wrists backward to my forearms in a very unnatural way.

Clutching my hands to my chest and unable to hold one with the other due to the dual injury, I ran to my coach, who did not see the incident but told me I would be okay anyway. Another round of icing, elevating, and ordering some wrist braces had me back to practice, but this time, I was not able to bounce back as quickly, and with permanently limited range of motion. We were in the middle of competition season, so my mom was instructed to buy guards for my wrists. I never took them off for tumbling or vaulting throughout the rest of my gymnastics career. Once again, no therapy or doctor's visits followed. This was just your regular workout injury that we pushed through. Just another day in the life of a gymnast.

Up next for my body that hadn't even hit puberty yet was an ankle injury. It was silly, really. I walked across an in-ground trampoline and rolled my ankle so badly, I couldn't even stand up to walk it off. For this particular injury, I was immediately taken to the doctor the following day, and I had a compression fracture on the inside of my lower leg bone, toward my ankle. I was casted for a short period of time, but we were able to convince the doctor to take it off early, so I could make it back in time for my first competition. No physical therapy involved. I did a million heel lifts and strengthening exercises, and I continued to tumble, now sporting a beautiful ankle wrap or athletically taped ankle for intense practice sessions.

This lack of full healing would lead to so much strife down the road. We had no idea I would never fully recover from this and would struggle for the rest of my career. At first, I just had pain in that same spot at night. Then it was during tumbling and running, and soon, I was limping at school or just getting around with sneakers on. This time, since there was no obvious single event to cause injury, we went back to the doctor, and I was found to have a stress fracture. No time to deal with that. My options were clear: deal with it or quit what I loved most. It's crazy to think that, sometimes, the things we love the most cause us the most pain. Guess what I did? I taped my ankle for every practice and pushed through. Quitting wasn't an option for me.

I'll skip over the multiple broken noses, injured elbow, and broken tailbone and jump ahead to the injury of all injuries. It was my senior year. I had reentered competitions after "retiring" at the ripe age of sixteen, returning later that year with unfulfilled dreams of competing as a senior. It was my first competition back in a leotard with my now older teammates, but this time, my high school friends, teachers, and family members were present in my own hometown to see what I had spent my life working for.

We had warmed up our first event, and I was in the middle of the lineup for the beam. I had a series of two connected flips, the first skills in my routine; they were fast-moving, one dependent on the alignment of the other to show connection and complete the move.

When it was finally my turn, my stomach did its own somersault. I stepped up, saluted, and mounted the beam. I stood up, set up to jump backward, and began the first flip of the series. I was so excited that I was off balance, but, as any good gymnast knows, the connection is key, so on I went into the second flip, way off from center of the four-inch target I was supposed to land back on.

Well, only one foot made it on the beam. As I tried to sneak my foot on in hopes of still getting credit for the set, the odd angle put pressure on the inside of my knee, resulting in me watching my knee fold inward as I landed with a thud on the thick mat under me. The rest is kind of a blur. I remember screaming for my mother and sobbing, as my school's athletic trainer rushed to my side. The pain was indescribable; it felt like my lower leg was no longer connected at the knee. Any movement made the pain exponentially worse. As they inflated an airbag-like brace around my knee, I could hardly sit still.

I was carried off, put into my mother's car, and told I wouldn't be able to go to the doctor until Monday. I would be completely broken for two whole days.

Not only did I break physically, but I broke mentally, too. All the work had been for nothing. The long hours and missed social events, the conditioning and stretching at home and on weekends, it was all over. The easy, the hard, the flying through the air to land like a superhero—it was all over for me, and I knew it before I even lay down that night. Not only was my career over, but I didn't even get to show off what I could do to my friends, who were finally able to attend a competition. They did get to see me scream my head off like a baby, as I cried for my mother in the loud and echoing ballroom of the hotel that had hosted the meet.

An MRI and doctor's visit later, the results were in: I had torn the medial ligament in my knee along with the quad muscle that anchored my knee cap in place. Surgery was an option, but they were hopeful for another, less-invasive option: physical therapy. I had no idea what I was in for.

Driving was out of the question, so I got dropped off at my first PT session, using crutches in, with my mother holding open each door for me. I clearly remember meeting Stacey, a really jacked guy who was way too excited to see the video my mom had happened to record of the most awful injury of my life. He was going to become one of my closest confidants and would guide me through a grueling journey of recovery.

He was there as I stared at my leg, willing my muscles to move. He was there over all the weeks it took to make a full rotation on the stationary bike in the gym. He allowed me to cry as I remembered I would never be a gymnast again. Something else he did was lead me to a working muscle, less pain, and lifting weights like never before. I got back to walking, running, squatting, and feeling like an almost-normal teenager, I just couldn't kneel or bend my knee all the way anymore, but I was on the road to recovery.

Stacey changed my life and showed me how to be a relatable and kind person who helped people get back to their lives. He was encouraging and upbeat, and he thought he was funnier than he actually was, but that made him lovable and a great motivator. It's crazy, because I never thought I'd want to be just like him.

Most physical therapists have been athletes. That, or they've been really into sports and are excited to help athletes. Most have experienced some kind of injury or setback to their own careers and want to work with the injured to get them back to their old selves again. This is exactly how it came to fruition for me, too.

Well, that and I was tired of working all those jobs, waiting for an opportunity to come my way. Instead, I made the opportunity happen. I finished the prerequisites I'd lacked, and, well, you know the rest.

Anyway, I was in. I was going to be a physical therapist.

CHAPTER 3

Love Your Neighbor

Mark 12:31: "Love your neighbor as yourself."

At first, this seems pretty self-explanatory, but I think it's important we define who our neighbors are. The answer is simple: they are everyone. Not so easy, is it now? Where do you start? Well, that's also simple: start with your next-door neighbor.

What is a neighborhood? Well, that depends. If it's 1960, then maybe it's a quiet street with cookie-cutter houses, perfectly manicured lawns, and children playing outside. Maybe it's a dirt road with a couple of acres between each front door, nothing but land and sunshine between each home. Or, perhaps, you're like me, and you live on a quiet cul-de-sac street with new families and new homes, waiting for memories to be made.

Maybe you knew the names of all your neighbors, too. Not only did we know their names, we knew that Chet, the retired army vet, spent most of his time in California and would fly back to Tennessee to spend a couple weeks visiting family. We knew that Toni worked as a nurse with a local doctor; she worked way too many hours because she was too good at her job. She was always the first to leave and the last to come back to the neighborhood each day. Chad and his wife Jill had only been back in the States a year after returning from working for the past few years as missionaries in the Dominican Republic.

Our neighborhood was one-of-a-kind, because we were intentional. Some may call it nosy, but we called it loving your neighbors in its purest form. Matt, our small group leader and contractor's assistant, who ended up loving the neighborhood and staying, created a chart of all the homes on our road. We all helped fill in the blanks, so we could get to know everyone better. This would eventually be crucial for the night that changed everything.

I didn't know who lived next to the people across the street from us, but I did know that Laura and Paul lived two houses down from us. My husband, Kory, knew Eric, who lived on the corner, and someone else had already filled in the other Eric's family's name next to them.

We created a diagram of Hensley Drive, and when that was done, we moved on to the newer cul-de-sac that was perpendicular to our street, Hensley Court. We worked on the names and members of each household, adding a rough background, like where they worked and maybe where they went to church. We did all of this because we cared. We wanted to put effort into learning about each family and, eventually, grow a relationship with them.

I remember thinking how exciting it was to imagine connecting on a deeper level with all of these people. I dreamed of group pumpkin carvings, movie nights (even though I hated movies), and meeting people in all different walks of life. I wanted to share gardening tips, hold a ladies' coffee once a month, and have a street to raise my baby with the other babies of the neighborhood. I wanted the real, heartfelt friendships I'd missed out on during my childhood.

* * *

Before we ended up in this perfect neighborhood, Kory and I lived in an apartment in town while he was in school. It was a beautiful new apartment with granite countertops and outside storage, only a mile away from his school and my work. We couldn't have asked for a better location. Since I was from Florida, where things were way more expensive, the price was a catch to me, too!

We moved in while the second building was still being constructed and waited over a year for the pool to be finished. We lived on the second floor and endured the upstairs neighbors walking with heavy footsteps, but we had the protection of not being on the bottom floor, with our patio less accessible to intruders. Kory and I moved in together after our wedding and quickly got to hanging up our nautical wedding portrait, arranging our hand-me-down furniture, and putting away our new dishes in the first place we'd ever get to call ours.

We embraced our new lives together and filled that apartment with friends, love, and memories, even letting a friend stay with us when she was down on her luck and finishing grad school.

We lived in that apartment for almost two years before getting the itch to start looking for a home to call our own. And truly, it's my fault it happened so soon. You see, I loved our location and affordable rent, but I was in my late twenties. I was over living the student-style life and hearing the younger groups come in and out at late hours. I would think to myself, "Don't you have a test to study for?" Man, I really was getting old, I would think. Plus, I wanted to start a family soon.

Okay, let's back it up. It was the Internet's fault, really. On my way home from work one day, I remember seeing a for-sale sign coming up on a nearby lot, and I just thought to myself, I wonder how much. From there, my sleuthing began. I began to obsess about pulling up mortgage calculators and scouring realtor websites. I even went as far as setting up some viewings.

Kory played along, coming to showings, giving his opinions, and he, too, began to see the dream with me. A few months in, we found the cutest two-story white home that was just borderline farmhouse-style on the north side of town. It needed updating, but it had a huge master bedroom and bathroom, a big green yard for future kiddos, and it could be ours. It was affordable and wouldn't be more than the monthly rent we were paying. Were we crazy? Or could our dream actually happen?

Well, just a few days later, Kory went to his childhood friend Chad's to help move a piece of furniture into the new home they had just bought. One of the benefits to having a truck was doing favors like these. Their house was on the opposite side of town, and the short ten-minute drive seemed like a lifetime away from my favorite grocery store and from our school and work.

While Kory was there, he noticed that their house was one of just a few on the quiet cul-de-sac, and he became curious as to the plans for the neighborhood and how we could acquire a lot. We were directed to the owners of the lots, who worked with a local general contractor to create great starter homes for young families and families-to-be, like ours.

At first, I was hesitant, because buying a home was one thing, but I had no idea what went into building a house. Little did I know, it was all different: the finances, the work, and all the unknown variables, but we were young and up for the challenge. Who cared if Kory was still in school? And while we're at it, let's get two German Shepherd puppies. Yeah, all of that seemed like a really good idea.

Thank goodness Kory's stepfather knew a lot about building houses and had contracted his own house, which was just a couple of hours away, where he and Kory's mom now lived. They agreed to help us on our huge endeavor. Oh my, my, my. We had absolutely no idea what we were getting into.

We met with our contractor, decided on a house design, signed for our lot, and we were off. From there on out, it was long nights of priming, painting, and painting another layer. We moved scaffolding, painted trim, hung doors, and painted some more. At one point, we had to bring in space heaters, because although the house was dried-in, and we wouldn't get wet from any potential rain or snow, it was so cold, the paint started congealing as we painted late into the night between study breaks for Kory and work hours for me. We brought those two new little puppies with us every time, though, and they snuggled each other and napped in their crate and provided great play and snuggle breaks for us.

We picked out discounted and discontinued hand-scraped hardwood floors. I remember feeling so amazed we were actually laying our own hardwood floors. Each staple I shot into the floor, with the careful guidance of my stepfather-in-law, of course, was just that much more addicting. Every swipe of the paint brush, every nail, every late night, and every ruined pair of scrubs I forgot to change out of continuously brought us closer and closer to our home—loving it, getting irritated at it for all the work required, and then loving it even more.

Through the skill of Kory's brother, plus the willingness of his mother and her husband to help us, we passed inspection, and less than a year after starting our endeavor, we were ready to move in. We had painted every piece of that home, installed every door and lock, nailed every piece of trim, laid every piece of hardwood floor, and set all the tiles in each beautiful bathroom. There is no labor of love like hand-building your own home. The best part of the whole experience was that Kory didn't fail out of school during our year-long endeavor!

It was only after we began the journey that we found out our neighbors would be more awesome than we could have thought. My friend Amy, whom I'd worked with at the hospital, had bought the house going up at the end of the street. Matt and his family would be across the street from Chad and Jill, and our great friends Kayla and Jon would buy a house just around the corner from us, followed by Brittney and Jared, also around the corner. God was slowly setting up our dream neighborhood. Already loving the neighbors whom we knew made us eager to meet the rest of them and bring them into our quickly growing circle.

* * *

As our neighborhood grew and grew, so did our tight-knit group, which evolved into biweekly meetings where we got together and shared a meal, shared our lives, and shared our ideas on the most recent Sunday morning lesson.

Our convenient small group was made up of most of my neighbors on our end of the street. This group was something new to me, as I had not been brought up in a church community with a regularly meeting group. I was still trying to find out how I fit in, since I wasn't raised in the church and had questions about things that other people took for granted.

I tell you this because I was unable to be at every gathering, due to work, and I was definitely a question-asker, which also made me feel kind of like an outsider, too. Well, at least at first.

These genuine and caring people took the time to answer my questions, help me process through my thoughts, and validate everything I felt. I tried to do the same for them, but I definitely was not the same person I am today. I'm so grateful for their grace for me during that time. These people helped create the person I have become and gave me a home in a group like I'd never experienced. They became my second family and truly brought meaning to what it means to belong to a community. They taught me to love people for who they were, not expecting them to change.

This group slowly evolved into the missing church family I never knew I needed. I craved our meetings, loved our discussions, and was able to really grow my relationship to God, because I was able to better understand His word and what stories the Bible could teach me.

Some nights, we would spend an hour on just a few verses, digging down deep into the history, original Latin text, and vocabulary, and we would link it to other texts throughout the Bible. This group taught me how to truly study the Bible and how much more meaning these phrases could have, when taken off a painting on the wall and dissected to their true meaning. We always ended each meeting with an application into our daily lives. How could we better live this meaning, day by day? This meant a lot to me, because it meant I was putting what I learned into action.

It also helped that we always had a full belly before our discussions. We did potluck-style meals, but Jill was usually the mastermind behind our gatherings.

One week was especially exciting to me, because we were having dinner two doors down, and it was omelet night! They'd had this awesome idea to make our omelets in a plastic bag, with all the ingredients mixed in, then drop it into hot water, and let it cook. It was amazing! Jill was always so good at thinking of these amazing ideas and then sourcing all the ingredients. The cheese, bell peppers, spinach, tomatoes, olives... It was all there! I was just sad that Kory couldn't be there too, because he worked a twelve-hour shift every other Sunday. I knew he'd have appreciated the bell peppers and black olives they had, since I didn't like them and didn't keep them regularly stocked in our own fridge.

As I walked back home that night, I thought of how grateful I was to have this neighborhood and this group, where we could be ourselves without being self-conscious or holding back my questions. I was just thrilled that people wanted to invest in me, to answer my queries, and help me on my journey to grow closer to the Lord.

I walked into my unlocked front door, where I was greeted with kisses and barks from Xena and Shadow. What good girls.

* * *

Oh Xena, I thought, as I got up for the fourteenth time that next night to let her out. She would live outside, if we let her.

I walked to the back door, where I let the dogs out and stepped out to join them. It was a beautiful night, so I walked over to my favorite place outside.

I loved sitting on my swinging bed that Kory and his brother had made for me. Kory and I spent countless nights with a big comforter, pillows from our bed, and sometimes the girls on top of us, just falling asleep with the fireflies and a gentle breeze. I took every opportunity to sit on it and just appreciate my life.

I walked out and sat down then very quickly stood back up. What in the world were the girls doing?

I opened the back door to the inside of the house and turned on the backyard flood lights to find the girls running patterns behind me. They were completely in sync as they weaved beautiful, long figure-eights in the backyard. It was almost like a dance as they trotted one way, turned in sync, and then circled back the other way, their coats shining in the light. They didn't bark, they didn't run with haste—they didn't even look at me. They just ran one way and then back the other for at least five minutes.

As I came out of my stupor, I thought of enough to record them for thirty seconds. It was so odd. They didn't stop until I called them in. It was like they came back to the present world and trotted back over to me then straight inside without another look back.

Strange. I wondered if kids were running around the neighborhood. Or perhaps there was someone creeping around backyards. We had noticed an increase in police patrol down our quiet street lately—perhaps they were looking for someone, and the girls had found them. There was that time a few weeks ago when some man, quite possibly under some kind of influence, found himself exposed and pressed against the sliding back door of our neighbors' house. Maybe it was going to be one of those nights, I thought, as I sent the video of the girls to our neighborhood group chat, just to settle my fears.

"Hey, y'all. The girls are acting funny. Is everyone okay?" I then sent a clip of the video of Xena and Shadow running through the yard.

"Everything is okay over here," everyone chimed in. I was nervous, because Kory was working that night, and I was home alone. If there was a creeper in the neighborhood, I wanted everyone to be alert and let me know things were okay. Luke, who lived at the end of the street with his new bride, Amy, texted me immediately and asked if I'd like him to come over and check things out. It was like he had read my mind.

"Yes, please, if you don't mind!"

Now, let me tell you a little bit about Luke. He was an army veteran who had hair brighter than Hensley sunrises and a soul with passion that matched his hair. He wasn't afraid to tell you what he thought and what he thought about your thoughts, but he was as loyal as they come. He was there when I needed help gluing Shadow's torn toenail together, the day she stubbed it on a rock while out chasing a squirrel, when Kory was out at work. He was there to help unload heavy loads, including the piano I surprised Kory with when he was away on a guy's trip.

He would even bring over gardening equipment, and he taught me how to mow the lawn one summer, to surprise Kory. Sometimes, he'd stop on his drive home just to chat, if he saw you in the yard. Coming over to check on a neighbor was as normal as breathing to him. If the world ended and I needed someone to protect my family or provide extra firearms, you could find me at Luke's house.

He walked around our yard and on the outside of the fence. Not finding anything suspicious, he came to give me his report. It was then that Jill chimed in that she was also home alone and locking her doors. We were so lucky to have neighbors to step in when we needed it.

CHAPTER 4

Fire Drill

Philippians 4:9: "Whatever you have learned or received or heard from me, or seen in me—put it into practice. And the God of peace will be with you.

God prepares us for all circumstances, whether or not we realize it. We are faced with situations we have been prepared for and have practiced for, in one way or another.

One week prior to the storm, I had a drill. Not like your typical school fire drill, because it wasn't planned and nobody gave me the memo that it was going to happen. For starters, there were no tornado sirens in the county, which I didn't even know existed at the time. Heck, we didn't even have a local news channel and relied on the Nashville coverage, where our town was usually only mentioned as an afterthought, and that was sporadic at best.

We had no idea how this "drill" would prepare us for the night it would matter the most. It would prove to be crucial to my ability to be ready.

Kory was working another twelve-hour shift at the hospital, so it was just me and the girls, hanging out on the pleather couches, snuggled up and listening to the wind pick up. The two German Shepherds didn't mind the rain or wind; they snuggled into me as we channel-surfed.

The wind continued to howl, becoming more intense, and I started to become nervous. I heard the grill shift on the covered back patio, just outside the living room windows. I knew I needed to go out and pull the pillows in, so we wouldn't lose them, because we all know that those suckers are expensive! Xena gave me an eye roll as I pushed her off and walked to the double doors, not expecting what came next.

As soon as I opened the door, I had to brace myself and grab the doorknob with both hands to prevent the door from slamming open to the back porch. The wind had really picked up and was starting to gust so hard, I was too afraid to even go outside. I planted my foot against the wall, leaned with all of my might, and slammed the door shut. This was unlike any other wind gust I had felt, even after growing up with hurricanes in Florida and typhoons in Japan. This wind was angry and unforgiving, and I was not about to sacrifice myself for a few pillows.

I don't normally call Kory at work, but I was getting nervous, and I didn't know what to do. Yeah, I needed his support, and this was urgent enough to warrant a call while he was on shift. I searched for my phone and pressed the first speed dial.

He picked up on the second ring, with a slight edge to his voice. "Babe? Is everything okay?"

"I'm okay, but I don't know what to do. The wind is picking up moving the grill around, but I'm afraid to go out there." He could sense the hesitation in my voice, which was odd, since I didn't startle easily.

"Well, try to pull the furniture and grill in toward the middle of the porch the best you can. It'll be okay."

"I don't know if I can. I barely opened the door and felt like I was being sucked out!"

"Just leave it then, and we will handle it later. The grill will be fine."

He always thought of my safety above everything else. It was really something I had taken for granted, but something that would come to mean everything to me.

"Go get a lantern from under the stairs, just in case the power goes out," he instructed.

Thankfully Kory and I had been on a purge of the house the past few months, and he had cleaned out the closet under the stairs the week before. It had become a part of our journey to declutter, to get rid of things we didn't use, and to create a more beautiful space to live in.

Brilliant, I thought. *He thinks of everything!*

I made my way to the half-bath under the stairs and yanked the heavy storm door open. I always forget how heavy that door is compared to the other inside doors. As I pulled it open, my hand was pulled off by a weight I wasn't expecting. I then slammed the second door open, because it wasn't nearly as heavy, as I opened up the closet.

Sheesh, could I be any more clumsy? I easily found the lantern, and I also spotted an unopened white box filled with the battery-operated flickering candles. I grabbed those, too, because I figured I might as well test them out and create some ambiance, in case the power really did go out.

I set the lights on the coffee table and went to search for the box of wine and a glass. That, of course, was a priority. I waited to pour it and decided to go try the back door again, because the sound of the grill scraping the pavement was really starting to rattle me.

This time, I was ready for the pull of the door, so I let it open just a crack and slid out, keeping close to the wall of the house. The grill had moved from the edge of the porch and was wedged up against the door, while pillows had been thrown all around. My flowing curtains on the porch were dancing in the wind, and the branches of the backyard trees were bent at odd angles.

I began to throw pillows and loose items inside as quickly as I could and then rolled the grille next to the hanging bed. Just as quickly as I'd come out, I slipped back inside. Then, I carried everything I'd pulled inside through the living room and mudroom and out into the garage. As I closed the door after my last trip with the pillows, the thunder started booming. Just as quickly, the power cut out.

Well, good thinking, Kory, I thought. I felt my way to the coffee table and turned on the lantern then began turning on my flameless candles. It was really quite beautiful with them all flickering their yellow glow.

Well, I thought, if this was how my night would go, I guess I should pour a glass of wine and settle in with the girls. There were no tornado warnings that I knew of, so I didn't feel the need to go into the safe room.

Let me back up. Said safe room was a reinforced half-bathroom under the stairs, in the middle of the house. It had plywood added between the drywall and studs to add an extra layer of protection. The door to the room was also reinforced and much heavier than your average door. All this had been done when we built the house, at the insistence of Kory; I had never given it a second thought before. Looking back, plywood seems so dainty compared to the winds that can so easily destroy them.

My brain is the exact opposite of a one-track mind. It wanders constantly. I can start by thinking of the beautiful flower I'm looking at, then digress to wondering where it's from, and then to thinking about the climate it's from, followed by dreaming of a tropical vacation and what Caribbean island I'd love to visit. One of my favorite things is to look back and wonder, how did I get here? Then, like a detective, I retrace my steps back to the original thought. Anyway, I digress...

As I started to think about our safe room, I thought of emergency things we may need. We had the first aid kit, two gallons of water, a lantern, and the obligatory box of wine to pass the time. Well, in an emergency, if I was home alone, I'd have to care for two German Shepherds. I love my girls, but there is no way I could manage both of them, if it was just me in a stressful situation. I'd need their gentle-lead leashes, the only way I could control two eighty-pound dogs with a desire to greet everyone with kisses as if their very life depended on it. If I had to go in there, I'd need to grab their leashes...

Yeah, that's a good thought, I said to myself, as I took another sip of wine. I'll just store that away in my thoughts for another day.

It wasn't long after the power went out that it came back on, and the candles were returned to their storage spot in the closet. The leashes remained untouched in the mudroom, and we eventually put the pillows back outside and rolled the grille into its usual location. The drill was over, and just like when practicing for fire drills at school, nothing had happened except everybody involved was inconvenienced by the lost time without power.

I didn't realize how important it had been to think through what I would need to handle the girls in a moment of action. Locating their leashes and knowing those would be a necessity would end up being such a big help.

Ironically, the gallons of water, the first aid kit and, yes, even the wine would not be nearly as helpful in an emergency, when everything was blown away except for what you were directly holding onto, and sometimes, even that doesn't stay.

CHAPTER 5

The Calm Before the Storm

John 14:1-2: "Do not let your hearts be troubled. You who believe in God believe also in me. My Father's house has many rooms; if that were not so, would I have told you that I am going there to prepare a place for you?"

God prepares our way, regardless of what we are faced with. Do you see the road he's laid for you?

"**M**an, it's really windy out tonight!" I say with a shiver as I hop in the back of Brian's Durango. He and Megan had come to pick me up so Kory and I wouldn't have two cars out, because Kory was going to meet us for dinner after work.

It was Megan's new boyfriend's birthday, and we were going to enjoy some wine and dinner at one of our favorite local spots, Spankies. Yes, that's right, this restaurant by day and bar by night was called Spankies. Despite the weird name, they had amazing food. Also, they had half-price wine night once a week, where you would get a bottle of wine half-off with the purchase of an entrée. That's the night we felt fancier than we actually were and let loose a little, picking the more expensive bottles.

I had originally known Brian through our Sunday class at church, which he and Kory led. It's where Brian and I had amazing scripture-based conversations. But that's a story for another day.

After Megan had spent almost three years in a relationship that didn't suit her, she got to know Brian at one of our many famous parties, held for all the big holidays, including my birthday. I told her all the time that I was responsible for their relationship's succeeding, despite the fact that Brian's mother claims that title, as well.

"Yeah, I think we're supposed to get some thunderstorms tonight, and there's a tornado watch," Megan responded from the passenger seat, sweeping her long, blonde hair over her shoulder. We had both dressed up for the occasion, because, as a physical therapist, it's nice when you're out of scrubs and have time to do something with your hair.

"Tornado watch—how is that different from a warning? And while we're on the subject, are tornado sirens even a real thing?"

I had seen them in movies, warning the community to take shelter in one of those underground cellars where the doors are always flimsy and the main character is able to yank the doors shut at the last minute, before the sky sucks up everything around it.

"Yeah, of course they're real. You won't hear them out in the county where you live, but I know they have them in town." Megan lived within city limits, which was only three miles from my house. I liked being in the county. We had more space between houses and fewer regulations to follow.

We looked up the difference between a *warning* and a *watch* on our phone and learned that a tornado watch meant the conditions were favorable for a possible tornado to spin up, while a warning meant one was imminent or had already touched down in your area.

Crazy clips of the *Wizard of Oz* and *Twister* faded away in my mind as we turned up the music and completed the short trip to the other side of town for dinner, where Kory met us after his shift at the hospital. I was glad he was going to be driving, because I had planned to split a bottle of wine with Megan. We would probably get the Cakebread Chardonnay, because the best time to buy an $80 bottle of wine was during half-priced wine night. Besides, it went perfectly with my favorite Chicken Dianne over broccoli. I didn't care if my favorite was a complicated order: the sauce was way better over a green vegetable than a plate of pasta, no matter what anyone else said.

After a delicious dinner, numerous glasses of wine, and a ton of laughing, we parted ways and spent a regular evening at home, getting ready for bed. I loved to stand at my vanity, which was perfectly placed just across from Kory's so I could watch him slyly in the mirror without turning around.

Just down the hallway was our walk-in shower and beautiful large closet. Kory really had spoiled me, because the closet shelves had the leftover hardwood from the floors we installed; Kory and his stepdad had pieced them together and bordered them with leftover trim to create a beautiful wall for my shoes. I had made specific requests at the height of each shelf, which not only made putting each boot perfectly in place very satisfying, but was beautiful to the eye, as well.

On the opposite wall, I had a bench under the window with beautiful gold-and-teal curtains and, to top it all off, I had a chandelier in my closet. It wasn't an old-fashioned one with a candelabra or fake flames; it was rectangular, with dozens of sparkling rhinestones hung to reflect light from within the strands. Kory's family always made fun of me for this, but ladies, let me tell you something, if you have the option to put a chandelier in your closet, do it. I smiled as I walked under the beautiful, sparkling lights every morning, which made me so happy, it was worth every penny of my birthday gift that year. Kory loved to watch me smile that big, cheesy grin, too, and I caught him staring at me from the corner of his eye multiple times. My closet was definitely one to envy, and it was my favorite room in the house.

After our nightly routine of washing faces, brushing teeth, and me grabbing one of Kory's soft, worn-out T-shirts, we climbed up into our brand-new king-sized bed—we had just upgraded to it—and called the girls to join us. After some snuggles with the Shepherds and giggles over funny stories from the night, we went to bed, with Shadow claiming half of my pillow and Xena snuggling at my feet.

I'm lucky I'm a good sleeper. And with a couple of glasses of wine in my system, as well, I quickly fell asleep and didn't move, not even when the girls got up to pace the floor at 1:30 a.m.

* * *

Green lightning. That's what Kory described it as. Later, we would chalk it up to transformers exploding in the distance, but I've come to find out, it's a common phenomenon to see before tornados and big thunderstorms.

I don't know what causes it or why it happens, but I also didn't get to witness it that night, either. Despite our blackout curtains, Kory told me it was the lightning that woke him up. He got up to peer out the window and see the anomaly.

As he lay back down in a dreamlike state, not fully awake but not really asleep either, our phones alarmed with a shrill noise and vibrations. It wasn't even two a.m., but my blood was pumping like I was getting ready to run a marathon. I sat upright in bed, as giddy and nervous energy surged through my veins.

A quick look at our phone showed *TORNADO WARNING* in bright, bold letters. There was no second glance, reading the details, or wondering what county they may have been referring to. There was no pause to consider if this was real or whether we should turn on the Weather Channel or perhaps the local news. There was no panic, no terror, and no question between the two of us as we caught each other's eye and knew it was time to move. There was only focus as pure adrenaline rose me from the bed.

"Grab our pants," I said to Kory as I scooped as many pillows off the bed as I could fit into my arms. I didn't even look back to see if he heard me. I just rushed to throw the pillows on the bathroom floor of the reinforced safe room. When we'd built this beautiful house less than two years ago, I'd thought we were prepared, because, with reinforced walls, what could get to us? At the time, it had been comforting to know we had somewhere to go in the middle of our house that would provide shelter and protection, or so we thought.

I then remembered the weekend prior and how I had thought it would be important to grab the dog leashes. I have no idea how it came to me at that moment, but my next stop was around the corner, past the living room and kitchen and into the mud room, where, thankfully, the leashes were in their usual space, still untouched from the weekend before, though, with my scattered brain, there was never any telling if things were in their rightful places.

Sprinting back through the kitchen and living room, after grabbing onto door molding to help speed up my process, I met Kory in the foyer and threw the dog leashes at his feet. He threw me my pants in what felt like a practiced exchange. He headed into the half-bathroom, and once again, my mind wandered. I remembered I was barefoot, and we would be sitting or standing on the cold bathroom tiles.

"I have to get my socks!" I yelled and jumped one foot at a time into my pants as I rounded the corner of our bedroom, raced through the bathroom, and entered my closet to grab my prized alpaca socks. They were pure alpaca wool from the local farmer's market, my favorite pair.

I hardly even heard Kory yell, "You don't have time!" as I sprinted away from him. Who was he kidding? Anyway, I hated cold feet, and socks were important. Besides, what did he even mean, I didn't have time? What did he know that I didn't?

You see, in Florida, you get days' notice before a hurricane strikes. You may not know how strong it's going to be or the exact location it will hit, but you have time to grab things like pants, socks, and a decent T-shirt. I thought of how silly his statement was and started to question why I was even running through the house like a crazy person.

Our brain does funny things like this to us. Instinctually, we react appropriately, and then we let our own mind talk us out of our gut feeling. *Don't do that.* We have a gut for a reason.

Kory was flushing the toilet as I ran back into the bathroom and pulled the heavy door shut behind me with a thud. He called the dogs to him as I took my turn to empty my bladder—this whole fight-or-flight was really more of a flee-and-pee-type situation. I knew I needed to be able to focus, so pee I did.

Shadow crouched to my right, in front of the sink and the cabinets that held my box of wine, two gallons of water, extra toilet paper, and a first aid kit. The dog leashes lay in the sink above her head. Xena was to my left, between the wall and the toilet, casually lounging on a pillow. Kory stood between the door and me, looking at nothing but blank walls as I pulled up my pants and turned to flush the commode. Then, time stood still.

It's not something you can imagine. It felt more like a dream than reality. The Earth suddenly stopped rotating, then it began to rumble like a large building when the AC unit kicks on. You know the sound—how it builds in intensity and volume, and then, at the last minute, it settles into a low groan. Except this time, it didn't settle. I know the noise was deafening, yet, when I play back the memory, I can hear no noise at all.

"It's here," Kory said. I remember it as a whisper, but my mind tells me that wouldn't have been possible, because, one street away, houses were exploding into the night.

"*What's* here?!" I'm not certain if my words were spoken aloud or if they are a distant memory I've created since then. But in less time than my brain had to process, we became weightless.

It was like in those Marvel movies, right before the entire battleship explodes, when time slows down and you see each piece of the building fly by. Or like the moment during the Tower of Terror ride at Disney, when the elevator hits its peak and begins its plummet back to the earth. It's that feeling of butterflies in your stomach as you expect something big to happen.

At this moment, Kory tackled me to the pillows as I simultaneously grabbed all eighty pounds of Shadow into my chest and wrapped my arm around her collar, and the world around us exploded.

CHAPTER 6

After the Storm

Mark 4:39-40: Then the wind died down and it was completely calm. He said to his disciples, "Why are you so afraid? Do you still have no faith?"

In the moment of the big event, whatever that looks like for you, we may not be aware of God's presence, but He's there. He's guiding our footsteps, preparing our recovery, and protecting us as we navigate this imperfect world.

I remember how the door that was supposed to keep out everything on the outside flew away, and with it, my sweet puppy slipped out of my grasp and into the night, despite my death grip on her. I remember screaming and being so confused about why I was eating dirt. I couldn't understand why it felt like I was being dragged across the water behind a boat, just like we used to tube in the summer on the lake.

I couldn't tell if I was flying or being crushed. All I knew is that Kory's voice had never sounded so deep and in charge, as he repeated at the top of his lungs, "I've got you, I've got you." I didn't care if the tail I was holding in my left hand was that of a dog with a heartbeat or not—I wouldn't let her go, either.

Three seconds later, it stopped. We were frozen, buried, coughing, and alive.

49

"Are you okay?!" Kory asked me after the world stopped moving around us. I wasn't sure if he was yelling, whispering, or gasping.

I felt nothing and everything all at once. Numb, perhaps. I had no idea which way was up and which way was down. I grasped a handful of a dog's coat in my left hand, held an empty dog collar in the right, and lay on top of what might have been pillows, with Kory semi on top of me and semi by my side.

"I... I don't know." I didn't think I was hurt, but I had no idea what had happened.

Kory pushed what felt like a wall off of us, and I tried to sit up. I felt my phone by my side, and all of a sudden, it was bright. I had been able to see just fine before he found the lantern, but now it was clearly bright. It was also deathly quiet, which was an odd contrast compared to the train that had just run us over. But just as that thought crossed my mind, the screams started.

Realizing you've survived something you don't even know has happened is the strangest feeling. You are completely present and hyper-aware of absolutely everything, despite your lack of understanding about what the hell just happened. I knew I wasn't dead and this sure wasn't heaven.

Being thrown back to reality, I spit out as much insulation as I could, but I just couldn't get the taste of cardboard, chemicals, and dryness to clear out of my mouth. I wasn't sure if I was okay, but I wasn't hurt enough to stop Kory, because the next words out of his mouth were, "I have to go."

They were words that had so many meanings all at once...

"I have to go help the people who are screaming at the top of their lungs, yelling for help, but I don't want to leave you."

"I have to go and I know you're okay, because we are connected as one flesh."

"I have to go, but I'll be back for you."

All the variations of what he could have said clumped into one singular moment of understanding. It was also in that moment that I realized the tail I had so desperately been grasping was moving. *Xena!* I grasped her by the collar, and, sitting up, I saw that my phone and the leashes were at my side. The mystery lantern that had landed directly in front of us was already in Kory's hands as he began the upward climb. I told him I would take care of Xena and stay right there. I didn't know what "right there" meant, but one step at a time.

I had a little more drywall to move off my legs before I was entirely freed, and I had to figure out what in the world I was going to do with Xena. The screams of my neighbors told me they needed more help than just Kory could give, and I would be of no use with a frantic German Shepherd at my side, protecting me from everything that was, wasn't, and might have been a threat. In that moment, I made the first of many hard decisions. I decided that I had to pick people over my dog.

My mind was still processing everything that had just happened. Not once did I think, "Oh, I just got hit by a tornado and help must be on the way, so I'll just lie here and wait with my doggo." I took the leash, placed the gentle lead around her snout, brought her nose to mine, and kissed her as I silently said goodbye to my second dog of the night, but this time by choice. I clipped the harness behind her head and tied her to a 2x4 that had been pinned between the rubble of what might have been part of my piano from the other room and what we would learn was a wall of tile across the house from the master bathroom. I then followed the way Kory had left, with my phone in my hand, using the flashlight feature to guide each step.

Once out in the open, I realized how absolutely freezing cold it was. There was so much blinding light, I had to shield my eyes as I dialed 9-1-1. *Why was there so much light?*

"911, what is your emergency?" a woman said in a calm voice. *Who could be so calm? Didn't she have any idea that we were barely alive?*

"We've been hit! We've been hit! Hensley Drive. Send everyone!" I don't know how much of my call went through before all service was lost and those heart-wrenching beeps indicated our call had been dropped. *Okay,* I thought, *at least I have a flashlight.*

Getting off the pile I had climbed out from under was the next challenge. I was so grateful for my thick alpaca socks at that moment as I tried to climb down the slippery slope of what used to be part of my house. I think I was walking down part of the reinforced plywood, and there is no logical explanation as to why I didn't rip my feet to shreds from nails and debris.

I made it to the bottom and looked up to see Kory at the neighbor's house, ten feet away, which should have been more like fifty to sixty feet away. He was carrying the graceful and limp body of our neighbor's oldest daughter. It was as if she was cradling him, her curls falling around his shoulder. He moved with grace and angst, handing her off to another neighbor who was working on placing other kids in a car across the street.

I looked back at the ground as I made my way over to Kory to begin helping with anything and everything. It was at this moment I realized that God was here and He was fighting for our survival.

In the aftermath of the tornado, houses became rubble, 2x4s became splinters, part of our closets had flown away, and the other parts were scattered all over the city. Wine bottles from our trip to Napa lay broken among the decorations that had been hanging on my walls. Children's toys from other houses had mixed in with our things. But, in the middle of all the chaos were two shoes: a golf cleat and a sneaker, both belonging to Kory.

They lay there as if someone had set them by the front door, ready to wear. As if expecting me. Without time to bother with laces and wet wool socks, I was glad they were six sizes too big. I easily slid them on and then continued on my journey toward Kory.

Frantically, I asked, "What do you need?" What a loaded question. We needed ambulances, cranes, bulldozers. We needed jackets, dry clothes, and a good night's sleep. For Heaven's sake, my husband needed a flipping shirt!

"I need shoes!" he immediately yelled back at me.

Of course, he did! I shuddered as I thought of all the cuts and pieces of glass we'd be pulling out of our feet later. I could give him shoes. In fact, I was *wearing* his shoes! I kicked them off to him and immediately turned around.

"I'm going to get more." Another loaded statement. If you've never seen a picture of the aftermath of a tornado, I encourage you to look it up. I've posted my personal pictures on my website, even.

There were piles of rubble in every direction. Houses had been reduced to matchsticks in the middle of the road. Belongings were everywhere and then for some, they were nowhere. Our next-door neighbor's home had completely disappeared, and there were almost no possessions anywhere nearby. The fact that I had found two shoes was a miracle in itself. I don't know why in the world I thought I could produce two more. But that doubt never crossed my mind.

I had turned around and started to take a few squishy steps in my thoroughly soaked socks when I happened upon two more shoes. A left and a right. Tennis shoes. *My* tennis shoes. The one on the left had the hole in the pinky toe still, and the one on the right was part of a gardening pair. One left, one right. Just lying there, ready for me to slip into. I didn't even have the capacity to understand the significance of finding another pair of shoes just waiting for me to need them.

For some reason, in the moment I slipped on my shoes, I realized what was happening all around me. I was freezing, because a temperature drop had followed behind the storm. I also realized that it was hailing. I had never been in hail before, and it was more annoying than anything. The small pieces of ice were short-lived, and then rain replaced the pellets, which was almost worse, as it absorbed into my husband's T-shirt, the one I had commandeered before bed. It began to stick to me, making a nice gooey mix of the insulation, dirt, and debris that clung to my skin.

I was so cold, I could think of nothing else. There were screams, glass, pieces of houses, and live wires everywhere, but all I could think of was how incredibly cold I was and how I would likely never warm up again.

At this moment, Kory appeared next to me, and all I could say was, "I'm so cold."

Without a pause, he reached down and picked up a raincoat off the ground and wrapped it around me. How was the inside dry? And how in the world did he find *his* rain jacket? For the third time in less than five minutes, we had been given another miracle. It didn't make sense at the time, and it wouldn't be until much later that I would realize how something so small could mean so much.

It was also about this time that I knew I could not be alone again, that Kory absolutely could not leave my side. "Don't leave me again!" I yelled over the rain to him.

"I won't," he assured me and grasped my hand. It was our special way to hold hands. Not laced, but standard-style, except my pinky was tucked into his pointer finger. It was special; it's a way we said "I love you" and "I'm here." It was so comforting in that moment that I believed he truly wouldn't let me go.

Kory knew that Luke was with Chad and Jill, because we had heard their voices on the west side of the street, so we decided to head east, toward Laura and Paul as well as Joyce and Joseph's home. As we started running, we saw Joyce and Joseph limping toward us. We ran faster. When we got to them in what felt like years later, a quick visual assessment told us they had not fared as well as we had.

If you've ever taken off stockings, peeling them down around your knee and then off, well, that was what had happened to her skin, at her right knee. I could see the muscles in her leg just as clearly as I had in anatomy class in grad school, except hers were red and attached to a living person. That was all I could mentally take in. As I shifted my eyes back into the rain, I immediately tried to help her.

Joseph was not much better off. Although we didn't know it at the time, his Achilles tendon, the big thick one at the back of your heel, had been severed, and his ankle was not functioning. They were both scraped and bleeding and in shock.

Joyce was unable to comprehend the words I said. I yelled at her through the wind, trying to get her to understand that I would carry her, piggyback-style, to save her leg, but she just couldn't process what I was saying. I kept trying to grab her arms and wrap them around my neck while leaning forward, but she kept releasing my neck and grabbing my waist.

I knew we would both end up on the pavement where there was nothing but glass and debris, so I tried and tried so many times to get her to move her arms, but she just couldn't. I took her arm and threw it around my neck then stood next to her, unweighting her leg as much as I could. We hobbled back to the west side of the road, where headlights were approaching us. That meant a vehicle was working. Despite the fact that the storm came from that end of the cul-de-sac, someone had not only found keys and gotten a vehicle started, but now they had been able to drive it toward us.

Of course, it was Luke. I'm telling you, if the world ended, which to us, it had, I wanted to be in Luke's corner. Luke had just bought a silver, lifted truck days before the storm. He needed it for his business to haul his trailer full of tools to each job site. Somehow, his keys were lying on the kitchen counter after the tornado ripped through his bedroom and garage. He was able to unhitch the trailer and drive the children and the most injured people closer to help.

That's where he found us. The front cab was full of eerily quiet kids, and there was mud everywhere. These were not just any kids; they were the kids of my friends, who lived on my street. In that moment, none of this registered. I just knew Luke was going to get these people to safety, and that was what they needed.

Kory had already gotten Joseph into the truck bed, so I helped Joyce squeeze inside the cab. At some point (the exact moment escapes me, and all these events have lumped into one memory), I remember hearing Jill's voice call out to me. She has pretty poor vision without her glasses, and those were not something she had grabbed before being buried in the rubble of what used to be her home.

"Lauren, I can't see! Can you take me to Chad?"

Now I had a new mission: to reunite Jill and the four-month-old baby in her arms with her husband and their almost two-year-old daughter.

I grabbed her hand, and, carefully, I physically led her while verbally guiding her through the rubble, around the fallen power lines, trying my best to look out for nails, as we headed for Luke's truck. I can look back and recall that that trek was maybe a few minutes long, but part of my mind pictures it like a tangled jungle, pushing through vines and watching out for snakes, just trying to stay alive.

When we reached the truck, I dropped her off. Kory and I said goodbye to our friends and off they went. I had no idea where they were going, we couldn't see any of the road, but they went, and I felt a sense of relief. *Okay, the first group was getting out of here, and they were going to get to help.* They had to.

Luke's truck made it through some of the grass and over some rubble before the tires blew out, and the truck became too badly aligned to drive. The adults carried kids and the rest helped one another. They made their way down the street to the McBroom Chapel Church of Christ. This is where they would meet up with the ambulances, which couldn't make it all the way to our street.

Kory and I took each other's hands again and moved forward, being extra careful of the live wires hanging everywhere. Wouldn't that be ironic, if we'd survived this huge tornado just to be electrocuted during our escape?

The next stop was Matt's home. Matt and Angela went to church with us and had three boys, the youngest just over one year old. I remember going through the front door and realizing that it was raining to the right and dry to the left.

All I could get out at this point was, "Water, please." Their eldest, Ethan, ran around the corner to the kitchen to get me some.

Sweet heaven, I had never been so relieved for anything in my life. The first sip, I swished and spat out. At first, I felt a little bad, spitting in their home, but then I realized there was no roof and the rain would surely wash my spit away.

Kory gave Matt a rundown of whom we had seen so far, and I asked for belts and hair ties. It was an odd request, but I had no idea how many tourniquets I'd have to make. Kory asked for a jacket, and I finally realized that my husband didn't have a shirt on and he might as well not even have had pants on, they were so shredded.

I should have felt a wave of gratitude as I realized he had put his own raincoat on me before he had anything for himself, but I couldn't feel anything. All I felt was the terror and determination about all the work we still had left to do.

You see, all this time, it had been just neighbors helping neighbors. There was no EMS, no fire trucks, no ambulances, no anyone except the people on the chart we had memorized.

Leaving Matt's front door, we walked across what used to be the street to find a young woman carefully crawling over a pile of rubble, calling for her son. "Aiden, Aiden. Call to me honey."

I remember it more as a whisper than a cry. It was like I had intruded on a private moment, and it was so hard to watch. I didn't have any children of my own at the time, and I could not fathom the emotions she was holding back and working through, the emotions we all were working through.

Kory and I joined the search, and there was Will. He and Sabrina lived across the street from us. My memories of the night's events have combined and blurred, so thinking about it is as if I'm watching myself from afar.

We all climbed over the rubble, trying not to slide on the wet doors and appliances and furniture that had been dented, shredded, and destroyed. How can you be careful, when each step may crush a baby underneath you?

And then it happened. I felt the slice of the nail from afar, like it had happened to a third leg or someone else's leg. It sliced through my shoe, through my wool sock, and up into the fleshy part of the middle of my foot. There was no pain and no stress, no fear of the nail. As I stepped off of it, my only thought was, *I'll have to have Kory look at that later.* But we continued on.

I looked up at one point to see Matt there, holding a spotlight and using his phone. How was his phone working? I didn't give it much thought at that moment, but we would later learn that the tornado had taken out the cell tower for the area, and most providers could not receive service. Yet, clear as day, I heard Matt's voice making call after call.

In the moment, I was annoyed. Looking back, it's clear that he was making the right phone calls and was our life-beacon to the outside world, calling in backup and our farther-out neighbors to come help. He also had light, and though we could already see before, now we could see better.

I turned my head to the left and saw a shadow against a tree... *Was that someone moaning?* There was no way I could get over there to help them and assess their injuries. The piles of things were too high and wide, and I could barely manage the pile I was on. The guilt of being helpless lasts a long time, and my mind has tried to shove this memory away time and time again.

When I looked back to the right, next to Will was another young man. He looked pretty dry and was wearing normal clothes, not pajamas.

"I'm Scott Michael," he said. "I'm a first responder."

I can't actually remember if it was Michael Scott or Scott Michael, but I distinctly remember it was a man with two first names. And if he had gotten to us, then others would, too. We were going to be okay.

And with this thought, I slipped away and went into shock.

* * *

My memory of events comes in pieces after this. The memories are accurate, but their order is slightly skewed.

I remember seeing Jared, my best friend's husband. I can't remember if it was as we walked up to the house—well, you couldn't really call it a house anymore—or right before, as we left Loren's house—well, her pile. He looked relieved as he saw us. I guess he'd seen what was left of our house and assumed we didn't make it. He suggested that Kory take me to Brittney's, but I was insistent we go and look for Xena first. I didn't even let myself consider that Shadow wasn't going to be around. Who knew how far she was thrown or if she was buried somewhere?

We walked two piles down the road, avoiding power lines as we went, and then I recognized the slight incline to the road in front of what used to be our house. There was no way to even see driveways because of all the rubble.

We walked up to where we thought we had crawled out, and I yelled, "*Xena!*"

Somehow, we saw the shadow of a head and two pointy ears pop up. She didn't bark or whine; she just waited as Kory climbed across the rubble, untied her from the 2x4, lifted her up, and handed her to me.

Somehow, I easily walked across the boards, doors, tile, and other remnants of what we'd built, the eighty-pound dog feeling like nothing in my arms. I was so worried about her stepping on anything that I carried and carried her until we hit some sort of grass. Then, Kory took my hand again, and we walked the 150 yards to Britney and Jared's house, which stood without hardly a scratch.

We walked up to her front door and knocked. When Brittney answered, her face told me she had no idea how bad things had been just around the corner from where her five-month-old slept. I'm sure I looked fairly discombobulated, in a soaking T-shirt, sweat pants, mismatched shoes, and a raincoat. I was freezing and covered in mud and all sorts of sticky things. I struggled to get my shoes off at the door.

"Don't worry about it!" she scolded me as I struggled to keep my balance.

"I'm so dirty! I don't want to get your house muddy!" It was all I could think about. I became obsessed with not creating more mess in the only space that resembled anything normal in my now uprooted life.

Brittney continuously tried to get me inside and not worry about the disaster I'd brought with me. I slowly began to shed the wet layers, fixating on the desire to be warm and dry. I needed to borrow everything: underwear, a bra, socks, clothes, a brush. Holy cow, my hair! I couldn't even run a hand through it, it was so tangled with debris.

I slowly started to realize I wouldn't ever be able to give her these clothes back, because I would have nothing else to change into. As I took off my socks, I realized there was no cut in my foot... I was 100% certain I'd stepped on that nail, but there was no blood, no cut, and nothing stuck in my foot. This didn't even register as significant at the time, but I would add it later to my list of miracles.

Jared had followed us back and gotten clothes for Kory. Then they left me and Xena with Britney and went back out, because there were still so many people unaccounted for, buried, and needing help, since assistance teams were still unable to get to our road. The single rescue worker we'd seen happened to live close by, and he had come alone.

The ambulances, we later learned, couldn't even get to our crossroad. We were all one another had. On the way back to our street, Kory and Jared ran into Chris, who had come running from the neighborhood down the street. He had seen our foundation and the destruction where our house used to stand and couldn't believe that Kory was alive.

Kory continued to help neighbors that night, breaking down doors and using them as stretchers to load up our friends into pickup truck beds that had arrived at the other cul-de-sac. Many people got to the hospital in this broken fashion, in the back of trucks, with neighbors, or via any way we could get them there, because help still couldn't get to us. The vehicles of our neighbors, our church family, were used as an emergency transport service that night. They showed up because they knew the back roads and were able to get around most of the debris to get as close to us as they could. They were able to get people to the hospital, along with over eighty other neighbors who needed medical attention.

Back in the safety of Brittney's presence, I don't remember the phone call well, but I used her phone to call our friend Kayla. She and her family lived another half mile away, and they had a young daughter, too. It was such a relief when she picked up the phone.

"We're okay, but some boards went through Emmy's room, and the basement doors flew open."

Thank God that's all, I thought. We would later hear their story, about how their doors all blew open as they huddled at the top of the stairs, unable to leave the landing, unable to get to their basement.

"Our house is gone," I replied. No emotion, just a statement.

"*Where are you?*" she all but yelled into the phone.

"I'm with Brittney, but Kory and Jared are still out there."

"We're on the way."

When they got there, Jon joined the guys, doing what he could, and we all sat on the living room carpet. I still refused to sit on the couch, so I wouldn't get it dirty, and I don't even remember the conversation. At some point, I called my mother-in-law, and she told me they were coming. She asked me what did I need.

What did I need? What did I need? I had nothing. I needed a brush, a toothbrush, a bra that fit, some shoes... I needed *everything.* I had no words, though, and it didn't matter. She would know what to bring. She always knew what to do.

While my friends sat there, trying to help me in my overwhelmed state, the guys had gone back to help the others. They started with the neighbors across the street. It was crazy that the structure of their home still stood, windows blown out from the pressure, while the house across from them, next to ours, didn't even have a subfloor left and had claimed the life of a baby.

One of the worst injured survivors was Laura. She was buried, couldn't breathe, and didn't think she would live through the night. Before the storm hit, she'd had even less warning than we'd had. She and her husband had been in separate rooms that night because of snoring, and as they were running to each other from opposite sides of the house, they were hit. She told me she had been sucked up toward the ceiling as she tried to brace herself in the doorframe, and then just as quickly, she was forced down to the ground, where she had been struck, buried, and impaled.

It turns out she did live, but with a punctured spinal column, partial paralysis, and a partially amputated foot. The physical injuries were nothing in comparison to emotional ones she would have to endure as she was transported over an hour away to a hospital, all alone. While in recovery, the pandemic would prevent her from having visitors, and she would have to endure the storms later that month all on her own, including a tornado that hit five miles away from her temporary home. Talk about emotional trauma.

Another neighbor who was transferred out of town was the baby girl of Chad and Jill. She wasn't even two years old. When I had glimpsed her in Luke's truck, she hadn't been moving. We learned she had been struck in the head while her dad clutched her throughout the whole storm. She would need a metal plate placed in her skull, and she had to be put into a medically induced coma for far too long. The family would also have to follow strict guidelines, and they could not visit the beautiful baby they had almost lost. Months passed without any sigh of relief from seeing her up close.

Living in a small town means that everyone at the hospital pretty much knows everyone else. So, our friends who were surgeons operated on our neighbors. Kory's coworkers then took them as patients, once they were transferred up to the medical/surgical recovery floor. When his coworkers found out which road had been hit by the tornado, all they could do was look at one another, seeing the worry in the others' eyes, as they thought about us and asked around if anyone had heard from Kory.

Leaving our street, Jared, Kory, and John made their way back to the house where I was sheltered, they were joined by Amy and Luke. I remember the relief I felt as each person entered the back sliding glass door, which faced the wreckage but had no damage, itself. We were all a mess, but we were alive and we were together. It was a weird sense of relief, because we could see one another and be physically there. We had all heard the screams of our neighbors; we had all endured the roar of the tornado as it sped over us. We all had experienced it and didn't need any words to fill the space.

"I'm going back to look for Shadow one more time," Kory stated. It was futile... She had literally been ripped out of my arms, and all we had was her collar and leash. But I couldn't say any of that, and it wouldn't have changed anything.

I watched him walk away from me, again, and if I hadn't been squeezing Xena, I wouldn't have let him go. I begged him not to leave me, but on a deeper level, I understood why he had to.

"I'll be right back," he promised. It's all I had to hold onto, so off he went.

He didn't have to walk far, though, because as he opened the front door and stepped on the porch, he screamed, "*Shadow*!!" And she was there, on the sidewalk in front of the house, tail between her legs, ready to dart away, until she caught sight of Kory.

She literally bounded into him, and Kory picked all eighty pounds of her up and carried her inside to her sister and me. The four of us embraced, and it was beautiful, peaceful even. We wouldn't have to endure the loss so many others were facing that night. But those poor dogs would never be the same again.

We used to take those two German Shepherds on lunch dates with us. They laid at our feet at the local winery as we sampled wine and cheese. But wouldn't be able to do those things ever again. Shadow became afraid of every noise and howl of the wind, while Xena became overly aggressive, almost as if to balance her sister. Who knew our dogs would be so greatly affected, just like we were?

* * *

After the instant rush in the aftermath of the first storm, we sat. We breathed. We looked at the people we had grown to love. That was, until we heard about the second storm cell headed our way.

I don't know who had service or who found out first, but all I could feel was sheer panic. We had barely survived the last one with only a few fully standing houses... What would another cycle of storms bring our way? Would the walls withstand the wind? Would the roof be sucked up? Where would we go in this house?

They guys immediately got to work, grabbing the two mattresses and placing them in the mud room next to the garage— the only room without a window. We turned the couches, and then we just waited.

It was still dark, so we didn't know how far the storm had traveled, but we did know we were all staying here, together. Just waiting. Our families were on the way, our neighbors were in the hospitals, we were without power, some of us without things. All we could all do was wait.

At some point, I had asked Brittney for a brush, but that had been pointless. I couldn't move it through my hair more than half an inch, due to all the debris it had accumulated.

Brittney gently took the brush from me and began the process of making me feel somewhat normal again. The tears rolling down my face were soft and without noise. How could I feel so empty after everything?

CHAPTER 7

Life Isn't Fair

Hebrew 6:10: "God is fair, he will remember the work that you do and the love that you show."

Yes, God is fair, but the world isn't always.

When you start your life as a child, you depend on others for your care and you learn early on whether or not that will be provided for you. If it is provided, you develop a trust with your caregivers—at least until they give you reason not to trust them.

I don't have distrust in my parents. I don't have a significant tragedy that happened to me growing up, and I don't have a dark secret causing someone else not to trust me. But I do have experience with becoming wary and learning that not everyone deserves trust right away. I think this is why I find it so important to be honest up front, and to be as kind as possible to my kiddos. This has applied to the gymnasts I've coached and to the children I've help through rehabilitation as a physical therapist.

My beginnings of distrust and understanding that life isn't always fair started when I learned about favoritism in sports. My mom and dad did their best to make sure my sister and I had equal opportunities in our home life. That may not mean we were treated exactly the same or got the same punishments or rewards, but that they were appropriate to the situation and consistent, for the most part. Things were kept pretty fair at home, but that wasn't always the case out in the world. That was a hard lesson to learn..

I was in middle school and a fast-rising gymnast in our local program. I was at the gym four days a week, and I was hooked. I remember being invited to join the older girls during their practices and thought it was the neatest thing to be invited with a few other younger girls. I had no idea I was being favored and that the older girls would grow to resent me for it.

Funny how I always classified them as the "older girls." I was closer in age to them than to the girls I had been grouped with, with some of the older girls being in the same grade as I, while some of the girls I spent most of my time with were my junior by three to four years. I suppose it had a lot to do with my size, as I was a tiny gal, and my later start to the sport. I didn't join the competitive team until I was almost nine years old, which many gymnasts will tell you is past your prime, and I had a lot of catching up to do.

It wasn't during my time as a "favorite" that I realized that things were unfair. It was when the tides turned and another girl became favored more. Decisions were made that weren't for the best of the team, but mostly for the best for one girl, and that girl wasn't me. I wasn't invited to our coach's house or to stay in her room during travel meets. Looking back as an adult, these may seem like petty moments, but they meant so much to me as a child. These were the moments that began to show me that life isn't fair.

This continued as I grew older, after I sought out similar-aged peers, but we never quite clicked. I always felt pushed out and outcast. I'm not sure if that was from grudges held about my own "chosen" status by being younger, but it was hard when I wasn't invited to birthday parties and get-togethers. This continued on into adulthood. Facebook is always the tell-all when it comes to feeling left out and finding out about these events.

A life-altering event came when my coach for my entire gymnastics career decided to leave the gym that we had called home and go to a gym with much less equipment, that was much farther from home, and was unable to sustain a team our size. Most of the younger team members followed, but most of the older girls stayed at our original gym. Out of loyalty, my sister and I decided to follow, but after a few months, we knew that favoritism continued, and we could not sustain the distance and environment we had been placed in. We decided to see what this new coach brought in by the other gym had to offer.

I remember his charming smile, his beautiful wife and their kids, and his promise to make us the best we could possibly be. At first, everything seemed to go great. We had a new warmup regimen, and his exercises and drills made sense.

But then, the fun slowly began to leave the sport. I couldn't pick the music for my routines anymore. I had to change the type of bar grip I had grown to know and love, and bars became impossible for me after the forced change. We stopped doing skills and routines for months, in exchange for conditioning and exercise, and I remember feeling so lost and dismayed at all the skills and capabilities I was losing.

Next, we lost our glamor. The glitzy, sparkling leotards were replaced with simple, no-nonsense outfits, because they wouldn't "distract from our skills." Our hairstyles had to be simple, and my fire grew slowly smaller and smaller. Gone were the glitter, personal flare, and excitement that surrounded competitions. I remember seeing my old coach at these competitions and feeling shunned or dismissed during hugs and greetings.

The final straw was when we found out the coach we had grown to trust and respect, the man we'd traveled with all over the southeast, was a wanted man. A fraud. An FBI fugitive. I have no idea how or even if the gym completed a background check on him, but we were all in shock.

He had faked his own death, and his wife had also recently taken out a million-dollar life insurance policy on him. The details were unclear, and there was a lot of hearsay, but it didn't matter. He was in prison now, and we were again left without a coach. My trust in coaches and non-familial adults continued to dwindle.

From then on out, each coach who came to try out our gym wanted more from me. They expected harder skills, more spotting, and I was given fewer choices. This meant I had less and less trust, until finally, I couldn't do it anymore, and I quit the sport I had spent so much of my life investing in.

I had already lost faith in the adults with whom I had entrusted hours and hours a week, so what would make me trust these new coaches? If I didn't feel like they were looking out for my best interests, how could I trust them to spot my hard tricks, care for my ailments, and be sensitive to my fragile mental state as a young, competitive gymnast?

At first, I was devastated. My life, my athleticism, it all felt like it had been for nothing. In order to stifle this great feeling of loss, I joined the swim team. I had never swam competitively before, didn't know the first thing about each stroke, but I was an athlete, and if my friends could excel in the new sport, so could I.

What had started as ankle rehab became so much more. Paired with the bleak outlook around our gymnastics coaches, the confidence and excellent record of the swim coach was oh-so-appealing. Not only that, but it meant I was part of a school team, filled with same-aged peers and people I was already close with. They were my math-team peers and many people from my upper-level classes. They were a team that welcomed me with open arms. And the best part was my best friend was on the team, too.

My journey in youth sports really taught me a lot of lessons, but the biggest one I learned was how *not* to be. I realized how important trust is to young, impressionable girls, especially when they trusted me to coach them, catch them, guide them, and flip them up and over four inches of equipment.

Something else my gymnastics career taught me was the importance of safety. We have only one body, and in my early twenties, I had already been filled with chronic pains and injuries from all the times I was told to "suck it up," "walk it off," and "you're okay."

I remember hyperextending my elbow, my knee, breaking my nose, getting multiple stress fractures, spraining my ankles, ripping my hands and wrists to shreds with bars, and sustaining injuries to my wrists that were always just written off as "not that severe." I felt like I was viewed as a wimp whenever I complained, so eventually, you learn not to.

This is not healthy in any mental or physical capacity, because you are taught at a young age to ignore those gut feelings that something just isn't right. You're taught to push through, even if it means you will make things hurt worse or longer. Even if it means you are creating a lifetime of problems for such short-term gains.

When I became a coach, I knew I would value my girls' bodies for the super-machines they were, while respecting their boundaries, creating a trusting environment, and preparing them in a way that would reduce injuries. You only have one body, and it seemed silly to waste it on a dream you held before you even hit puberty, which was always so delayed.

My childhood taught me that that life isn't fair, because we live in a sin-filled world. It wasn't fair that my gymnastics career was cut short. It wasn't fair that my perfect neighborhood was destroyed. It wasn't fair that innocent children had to die. It wasn't fair that we had to face the destruction and years of recovery that lay ahead.

The world doesn't care about fairness.

CHAPTER 8

Preparation

Deuteronomy 31:8: "The Lord himself goes before you and will be with you; He will never leave you nor forsake you."

God prepares us for all challenges and trials and then leads us through the toughest storms we face. We are never alone. God prepared my life in so many ways before the storm, but it wasn't until a long time after the storm that I was able to look back and see all the ways He intervened in my life.

B oxes. Boxes filled with things that I hadn't even bothered to look at in over ten years. Boxes that had traveled with me from closet to closet, from my parents' home to every dorm room and apartment in college, to grad school and, finally, laid to rest in our new home. Who knew what was even in those containers at this point?

The worst part wasn't my boxes. No, the worst part was the boxes had doubled when I got married and inherited all of Kory's boxes, too. They were such a burden, taking up half a room upstairs. Things like old trophies, photos, sorority stuff, Kory's karate belts, my competitive gymnastics leotards, birthday cards from twenty years ago—things lost from all memory, collecting dust, and taking up space.

Maybe it was a New Year's resolution. Maybe it was the rising popularity of Marie Kondo's minimalist movement. Maybe it was a desire to make something of this cramped room. Whatever it was, we were finally ready. Kory and I spent a few hours each night after work, going through each and every box. We read old diary entries, looked at old photos, appreciated report cards, admired trophies, and came to terms with the fact that we weren't each other's first love through old letters. It was so liberating to get to know my husband as a child and young adult. Learning his likes and dislikes, watching emotion come over his face as he re-lived a memory—it all was a gift that I didn't realize I was getting at that exact moment.

We laughed, cried, and got very frustrated with each other as we decided what was to be kept and what was going to be donated or discarded. He was mad that I didn't want him to keep the bracelets he made while on mission in Haiti, even though he hadn't even known he'd still had them. He was frustrated that I had so many damn notebooks, many of which were only half filled, so I didn't want to throw them away.

There were *so many* folders from grad school and so many school books. Horrible memories from financial accounting class came rushing back, as I remembered the weed-out course that certainly didn't help my GPA. Each bag of trash or pile of things to be donated lifted our hearts a little more.

Then, finally, we were done. I sold the keyboard I'd gotten as a gift from my mother and no longer needed, now that I had a beautiful whitewashed piano downstairs. We donated organization bins that had been collecting dust, and we stacked all the books we had taken out of boxes to place up on shelves.

I used to take a lot of pride in my book collection. I had the original hardback *Harry Potter* books, some Bible-study material, and plenty of Bibles to go along with them, Jodi Picoult books, and

Nicholas Sparks books. Of course, there were the school books for physical therapy, too. I couldn't get rid of those, since I kept practicing. We organized them by genre, size, and aesthetics. We had one of those cool modern bookshelves that had empty boxes at different levels that really made it fun.

Once the boxes were gone, the books put away, and a desk placed in the corner, we began dreaming. On opposite sides of the room were two small alcoves where we would create a personalized space for each of our future children. We would put teepees, beanbags, shelves, and blankets so they would each have a space of their own, with a light they could control by themselves.

* * *

Our organization and cleaning phase didn't just end there. Although I didn't consider us to be packrats, we were very reluctant to throw things away or donate them or get them out of the house, on the off chance we might need them in the future and have to either repurchase them or go without. The most obvious was my own clothing stockpile.

The house plan we had decided to go with when we began to build had two walk-in closets per upstairs room. One was supposed to be attic space, but we had decided to enclose it and add a door, to allow for more storage. This ended up being a blessing, because it meant we had space for all of our stuff and, more importantly, all of those clothes I would eventually wear again.

Yeah, sure, girl. Those short-shorts from high school that wouldn't even slide up one of my thighs now—I'll keep them, because I was going to get fit again and somehow squeeze into my size zeroes. Yeah, unlikely.

Those prom dresses were staying upstairs, because who knows when I'd be invited to a snazzy event. I had shirts and jackets of every size for every occasion. I had been to leadership conferences, so I had business suits. I had jeans in every length imaginable. I would not accept that those chinos would never come back in style.

To make it all exponentially worse, and in my eyes better, my mother-in-law gave me all of her beautiful hand-me-downs. If shopping could be a form of stress relief, this woman should be as stress-free as they came. She always dressed to the nines in amazing brands and with impeccable style. Because of this, I never wanted to get rid of anything she gave me. Even if it didn't entirely fit, I knew it would someday, wink, wink. Well, I had White House black-market hand-me-downs, LOFT hand-me-downs, and other brands I didn't even know about.

And then, my mom and sister, bless them, too. We all have the same size foot, so when they bought shoes and stopped wearing them, I would come over, proclaim my love for them, and end up with a new pair of shoes!

What I'm trying to say is that I had a lot of clothes, and most of them would never make it out of the house on my body. I really hated to just have them sit in a storage bin as they waited to be sorted and then added to some rack, so I just hadn't brought myself to get rid of them quite yet.

For some reason that summer, it was time. The great closet purge of 2019 was underway. As a young professional and as I slowly matured and grew out of the college-girl persona I had been stuck in, I knew it was time to release all my beautiful, and perhaps a little too-short, sundresses, give away most of the suits, and find new homes for things that didn't fit my lifestyle anymore. Florida and Tennessee had many different styles, and the strapless dresses and spaghetti-strap blouses just didn't work here like they did there.

This is where God brought me Kinsey.

Bless this small-town, hot mess of a girl. I met her before she could even legally drink. Before she had graduated with her bachelor's degree, and before she had stopped dating our mutual friend.

After their break-up, she was always seeking my opinion of their latest conversation or text exchange, and I was happy to give it, because I saw something beautiful in her. She was outgoing, pretty, fit without being obsessive, smart (too smart, really), and driven, and she was in need of a big sister. You see, Kinsey was an only child, and although she didn't act like the stereotypically selfish and perhaps a little naive girl you may be picturing, she definitely didn't understand how to have girlfriends yet. She needed me, and I needed her.

Kinsey became the first young woman I was blessed to influence and help navigate through rough times with a kind but firm word of advice or to support through the relationships and misunderstandings with her coworkers. She gave me the confidence that I could really make a difference in people's lives, and she kept me feeling young, as cliché as that sounds.

Well, I decided I wanted to give to her my Lilly Pulitzer, Calvin Klein, LOFT, J Crew collection of clothes that were a little snug on me. She had an entrepreneurial spirit and was dreaming of law school, so I know she would love the suits and would have plenty of opportunities to wear them in the future. She was also an amazing cello player and played at weddings, so those fancy, understated dresses were right up her alley!

Kinsey and I spent hours trying on clothes. Well, she tried on clothes. I got to be the big sister, zipping her up, complimenting the fit, and watching her glow, as she twirled in front of a full-length mirror. It felt so good to be a part of these moments with her. It felt even better when I saw her out in public, wearing some of them, or in her profile on social media.

Although it wasn't the first thing that I thought of on the day we lost everything, I would eventually come to appreciate the fact that at least some of my beautiful clothes had been spared the fate of being ripped, ringed, and stained.

* * *

If you've ever had a wedding shower, or any shower of the gift-giving nature for that matter, then you know what it's like to get a random gift you'll never, ever use. That doesn't mean you don't appreciate the thought behind the gift. But, as humans, we are all different, and that means we have different expectations and needs. And some of us don't really want to use a $120 vase on the regular.

Yup. We got a beautiful, white, water pitcher from an out-of-town boutique as a gift. It was a late gift, and we didn't receive it at our shower, so I don't even clearly remember who gave it to us. When I opened it, I remember thinking it truly was beautiful, but not something I'd use at this point in my life. Soon after, when I was able to go to the little store to exchange the item, I learned of its astronomical price tag.

Holy cow, I was glad I'd brought this back and didn't just let it sit in the back of a cabinet somewhere, where I'd likely break it, anyways.

I browsed and browsed that store until Kory's last nerve was long gone. In a store that sells an expensive water pitcher, you can just imagine all the beautiful home things they had for sale. As a newlywed, you can also imagine the overwhelm I felt, wanting all of it, but not needing any of it. Wrong time in my life, I suppose.

Well, just as I was about to give up, I saw these beautiful, luminescent white serving dishes. They were perfect! They would hold food, so they had a purpose; they were kind of shiny, so I loved them; and they were on sale, so I could have both! They would still be the most expensive things I had in my kitchen, but they would go well with the China set I was hoping eventually to accumulate.

Well, let me tell you what. I got those suckers home, and do you know that they did? They sat in the back of some cabinet.

Yup. They might as well have been an expensive water pitcher. When we moved into our new home and I unpacked these beautiful dishes, my friend Megan happened to be helping. She mentioned how pretty they were, and just like a good pair of shoes I no longer wore, I asked if she'd like them. She gratefully took them.

Again, another blessing, that such beauty was spared our disaster. I think the most beautiful part of this story, though, is when it came full circle.

After the storm, we had our house-warming party to celebrate restarting our lives. We hardly needed an excuse to have friends over for delicious potluck, good music, better company, and a chance to just be around all of the amazing people in our lives, but this was a symbol of our fresh start.

The best thing about our parties or get-togethers was bringing friends from every part of our lives together. Our intimate friend group, our church friends, our work friends, our neighbors—the list is endless. I can't tell you how many awesome people (including some now married folks) we have brought together to become friends through our parties. We always tried consistently to be the same people, just trying to do the right thing in every aspect of our lives, so it never felt like we were acting or pretending with any of them. We all just existed.

Anyway, we were having our friends over for the first time in our beautiful new home. When Megan and Brian came over, Megan gave me a bag. It was nothing fancy, or maybe it was, and I just don't' recall, but I pulled out two beautiful dishes. They were white, chevron, and slightly sparkly, without a flaw to be seen. Our wedding dishes!

She had saved them and thought they belonged back in this home. It was so beautiful to see them come full circle. But let me just be honest: they are still sitting in my buffet, waiting for the perfect dinner party to be used! Insert laughing-crying emoji here.

CHAPTER 9

Daylight

John 11:9: "Anyone who walks in the daytime will not stumble, for they see by this world's light."

God will illuminate the path he creates for us. It won't always be easy, and we may walk through struggles and difficult times, but His plan always results in goodness and the best possible outcomes, despite the destruction that may lie in front of you.

After the second scare, which resulted in high anxiety, more rain, and not much else, we just sat there. We sat in silence, but we sat in the company of each other. There were no words necessary, and really, no words were available, as we sat and processed the past five hours of pure chaos.

Those who remained were relatively uninjured and didn't require immediate medical attention, but we had all seen those who did. We had heard the screams, the cries, and the pleas for help from our neighbors and friends.

I sat there, mostly numb, thinking, "What next?" because, in reality, where do you go from here? Our families were on the way to us, but who knew how long that would take? We knew that even emergency response vehicles couldn't get to us, and without cell service, we had no idea how far the damage had extended in our small town. We knew at least a dozen people on our street required immediate emergency medical care that would likely require them to be transferred to larger hospitals for higher levels of care, instead of remain at our single regional hospital.

We were all as dry as we could be, and Brittney and Jared's living room was in chaos, with three large dogs, four adults in mismatched clothing, two adults in their own clothing, and a baby sleeping in her room. We were surrounded with mud and debris, mattresses, pillows, and blankets tossed around the room. We were surrounded by our thoughts and the silence. What could we do?

At one point, I remember thinking that it hurt to turn my head to the left, to look out the sliding glass door and watch the sun come up, but it was hardly an emergency. There was no way I was going to the ER while the real injuries were being treated.

As daylight broke, we knew we had to go see what was left not only of our home, but of our street. It was surreal to contemplate, and I don't even think we knew what to expect. Kory and I stood up, joined hands, and stepped off the back porch.

How do I describe that walk? The sun didn't shine and the clouds did their best to conceal any light or hope as we crossed through two backyards of houses still standing. You have to walk up a very slight incline to reach my street via the back way. As we did, I turned and sobbed into Kory's shoulder.

We'd all begun the walk together, but the others hung back just a little as Kory and I breached the street together. It was devastating, and that word doesn't even begin to describe that full view of the aftermath of the storm.

Most of the houses were gone, and the ones that remained would have to be demolished or completely gutted. The home where Kory had ripped a door off the frame still stood, but the windows had completely blown out and there was glass everywhere. Debris was embedded in the walls and in the appliances, and it was soaking wet. Matt and Angela's home had half of its roof missing, which is why it had seemed like it was raining inside, the night prior, when they gave me that blessed glass of water.

Across the street, every single home was gone. Not a single 2x4 board stood in its original spot. That entire side of the road had been obliterated. Our house was the only one on that side of the street that even had wood and tiled floors left. Everyone else's subfloor had been ripped up, leaving only mud under the concrete cinder blocks that used to be the foundation.

It was hard to tell which lot had been ours. If I hadn't known the geography from where we were walking, I would not have been able to find it. It was a big scattered pile of stuff. Some of it was mine, but most of it came from the houses next to us.

It still was difficult to see, given the clouds and limited light, but we had to search for Kory's gun and wallet, which lay at the bottom of the pile we had crawled out from. I remember the triangle the 2x4 had created, allowing us to crawl out and then rescue Xena, so we began to search for it. We had to walk up a pile of debris and then walk down to crawl into the hole. As we were contemplating the best way to go about our mission, we were stopped by two young men in heavy-duty work clothing.

"Hey, y'all, you can't be over here." They said this kindly but firmly, and at first, I was confused.

"Why not? This is our... *Was* our house," I retorted. I could be sassy even after an event like the night before.

Their demeanors instantly changed as they realized we were survivors. "You lived here?"

Well, we used to, I thought. They then began to ask us about the night and who we could account for and who still needed to be found. They also relayed to us that they were guarding our properties to prevent thieves from rummaging through our now exposed homes and belongings.

My heart softened as I realized this. I also became sad as I understood they were not keeping us from our piles of rubble just because of the danger of the collapsible piles or hiding septic tanks that could cave in. They were also looking for people.

Wait! *They were looking for people!* They had *no* idea who lived where, who was in town, who had been taken to the hospital, and who still hadn't been found! *We could help!* We had made and learned the chart of the neighborhood!

This was the first true ray of hope I had felt in over twelve hours. It was an odd, foreign feeling when a smile came across my face. God had used the love He had created in our hearts for our neighbors in preparation of this moment, and we could now share that to help find people.

"Well, Chet, he's out of town in California, because he lives there half the time, so you don't need to look for him. Then Joyce and Joseph and the kids are all okay. We saw them last night. And I know Laura was alive, but I don't know if they got her out."

They had rescued her, he told me, and relief flooded my body. We didn't know the condition of the people on the street perpendicular to our road that fed off the main highway, but we could at least tell them how many people they were looking for and their names. We went through each house or, rather, each driveway, and the responder took notes.

After the whole ordeal, he explained to us that it was very dangerous to be on the properties right now, until they knew the extent of the damage of power lines and electricity, etc., and they were also going to systematically move debris and didn't need or want us in the way.

In other words, they were going to start looking for bodies. If things had traveled miles and been blown all around, there was no telling who they would find where. They didn't want us to witness that. And after everything we'd been through, it would have been too much.

Of course, I didn't realize the code they were talking in at the time, and Kory had to explain to me later what they were really doing with the machines they were going to bring in. I also didn't know what all the symbols in red spray paint stood for in front of each driveway. The circled numbers with an "x" drawn through. Kory had to explain that, too.

We made our way back to home base, and, to be honest, I have no idea what we did for the next few hours. Kory tells me I tried to sleep, which would make a lot of sense as to why I have no memory of that time.

Our brain is a funny thing. Memories can be altered, especially over time, and our body does everything it can to protect itself from harm, whether that harm is perceived or real. Protection from memories is necessary, too. I'm sure many of my memories and stories have a spin that is unique to me. However, that's really all I have to go on. My story won't be the same as my neighbor's, there may be gaps, and something may be completely eliminated from my memory. But that's what makes each person's memory unique.

* * *

I don't remember the amount of time that passed after we got back to Brittney and Jared's house, but Kory's family eventually made it to us. The hour-and-a-half drive had turned into a four-hour drive as they struggled to get around roadblocks and find someone to hear their story of how they were trying to get to us, because we had nothing and needed them.

It was an odd meeting, and I remember the hugs and suitcase full of clothes. I found a pair of jeans, only a little bigger than what I normally wore, and borrowed Brittney's boots, wearing a pair of wool socks so they wouldn't slide off my feet. We then began the walk back over to where our house used to stand, this time armed with our family. We were going to try to get a few things, look for Kory's gun, and show our family what we'd lived through.

As we ascended the small incline for the second time, I didn't stop as I heard them gasp. The beautiful blue home with light-gray roof and beautiful front porch was gone. The large red, white, and blue bunting flags we had hung from the porch plus the American flag and its pole were gone. And our white wooden rocking chairs were nowhere to be found, likely miles away in splinters.

The home that Kory's mom, Cindy, and stepfather, Kip, had spent months with us building and the one his brother Kyle had helped install stairs and trim on, it was all gone. So were the doors I'd painted by hand and the decorations that had taken years to accumulate. The hardwood floors I had personally nailed down, not once but twice, after a water leak happened five days after moving in, they were gone, too: water-logged and unrecognizable.

As our family sorted through what had happened in their own minds, I remained silent and kept going.

We walked with our family up to what used to be the garage, and, would you believe it, our YETI cooler hadn't moved! I don't know how we'd missed it the first time, but with more light now, we could really see. We had invested in one of those hardcore coolers last year, because we travel to Florida multiple times a year to visit my parents, and while we're there, we buy fresh fish off the boat around the corner from my parent's home. That thing was a beast, and, obviously, it could withstand a lot.

Our deep freezer was also there, although it had been moved away from where the wall used to stand and the top had been opened and gently flapped in the wind. We headed over to find our meat was still there, too! The venison and fish filets had weathered the storm! The top half had already begun to defrost, but the bottom stuff was still salvageable!

We grabbed the sixty-five gallon YETI and began to salvage what we could. It seemed so important at the time.

During our raid of our belongings, another pair of workers came up to us to tell us the same story as had the previous two. We knew they didn't want us there for mental and physical safety, but we really wanted to get a few things together, if we could. The compassion in their eyes was touching, and they told us to be quick, they would give us a few minutes. We salvaged some meat, our cooler, a few bottles of wine that had rolled out, and maybe a couple of other knickknacks that I don't recall. We didn't find Kory's gun, not any of them actually, nor his wallet. We didn't find my purse, either.

When we got back to our home base, we received word that our church had booked a block of hotel rooms for us. Before we even knew that we needed shelter, it had been provided. The best part was, we would all be right next to each other. It would be our transplanted street, all of us on the same floor. Well, except for those still in the hospital—and that was half of our street. What a relief, and one less thing I had to worry about. We had nothing else to do on that sad, sad street, and our entire neighborhood had lost power, so we decided to head out.

With our borrowed clothes and suitcase, YETI, and salvaged wine, we realized we'd need to walk to our family's vehicles, because our roads had been closed off to avoid gawkers, robbers, and the general mass of people who would soon hear about the catastrophe.

We began the walk just three blocks down the road, and I was so tired, I struggled to keep up, even though I wasn't carrying anything. I hated walking, even when I had clothes and shoes that fit, much less the weight of the world on my shoulders. As if reading my mind, someone who lived close by drove around the corner at that exact moment and let us jump in their backseat—another beautiful blessing—and they drove us down the road. God is always looking out for us.

When we got to the car, we piled in and were led out of the neighborhood by the parade of our family's cars. I don't remember whom I rode with, where I sat, or what I specifically saw, but I remember the feeling as I viewed the destruction that had affected so much more than our little street.

The line of cars we passed that the police officers had stopped was unbelievable. I wasn't sure if they were there to gawk, get to their home, or were unexpectedly trying to pass through a destruction zone. Whatever the reason, I was glad our lot, filled with things exposed to the elements, was being watched over.

* * *

By noontime, we were starving. There was nothing we could do at that point, though, because we couldn't check into hotels yet, so we decided to go eat. I don't remember who picked the restaurant, but we headed downtown.

I walked inside a local restaurant and requested a table at. I remember feeling ridiculous in my oversized clothes, and I mentioned to the waitress that we had just survived a tornado. I remember the confused look on her face as she pushed some tables together outside, as it turned into a beautiful, bright sunny day.

I knew it was a Tuesday, and I was alive, and I wanted a cocktail. It's strange, looking back, how I was concerned about what my in-laws would think about my drink of choice, or how I prepped my mind for having to explain to the waitress that I didn't have my ID. Thankfully, the bartender knew us.

We were granted our small reprieve from the craziness of the day: Kory and I had two drinks each. I could barely touch my favorite pasta dish, though. Who could eat at a time like this?

CHAPTER 10

Renewed

Psalm 43:3: "Send me your light and your faithful care, let them lead me."

God always cares for His people. He uses His other people to provide for us here on Earth.

After lunch on the day of the storm, the events became blurry in my mind. Some of it was from the drinks at lunch; some of it was my own brain operating on almost no sleep and in survival-mode.

I know we went back to our friends' home to pick up the girls and head over to the hotel, as they were graciously allowing our pets to stay with us. Our cousin met us there and dropped off a car for us to borrow -another blessing. Kory's eye had started bothering him, and we feared he might have glass or something else stuck in his eye, so we made a note to stop by an eye doctor and have him checked out.

We got checked in and headed to the elevator, holding the foreign bags our family had brought for us, a random assortment of things thrown together in haste. I realized that Xena and Shadow had never been on an elevator before—this would be interesting, but it wasn't any sort of event. They both timidly followed us into the big box and heeled at our left side. The jarring of the elevator doors and screeches as we came to a halt at our floor were nothing compared to what they'd been through less than a day before.

As we opened the door to our temporary home, the girls bounded in and claimed the bed closest to the window, immediately settling in together and falling asleep. Seeing them there, lying close enough to be comforted but not close enough to touch, Kory and I felt the smallest sense of normalcy. Our girls tolerated each other and loved being with us. That was enough to settle them in, as they no longer had to function on high alert.

Our family helped us carry in our luggage and then left us to recover and process the day. Then, they returned to their homes, promising to see us the next day. We began to look through our new things, finding toothbrushes, a hairbrush, and some underwear. We got out some comfy clothes, included sweatpants, a T-shirt for me with the ill-fitting bra I already had, and Tennessee Volunteer-themed shorts and sweatshirt for Kory.

Up next: the shower. We longed for it and yet, at the same time, dreaded it. I knew we were covered in every sort of debris imaginable, but the adrenaline of the night and morning had not yet allowed our bodies to reveal the minor aches and pains associated with getting hit in a head-on collision or buried under your home.

Kory and I went to the bathroom, carefully helping each other peel away layers without getting debris everywhere, avoiding cuts and caressing bruises. It was the first time we had seen each other without clothes and in the light. As Kory gingerly peeled away his shirt and shorts, I gasped. I had forgotten that last night, he hadn't even had a shirt on when we'd been hit. His pants had been tattered, and he had used his body as a shield over me when our house had fallen on top of us and we were dragged across the yard. He had deep scratches down his left tricep, trunk, and left thigh.

The bruises were starting to take on deep purple hues. As all of our adrenaline subsided, he began to feel the soreness.

Sometimes, I see those pictures on my phone, or a memory will pop up showing me his injuries, and I experience two emotions. The first is overwhelm at how much this man loves me and that he didn't even think twice as he shielded me that night. The second is a shudder, because I remember seeing those injuries for the first time and being overwhelmed with sadness at the thought of him being so hurt.

Don't get me wrong: we had neighbors who were in way worse shape. They had to have surgeries, lost the ability to walk, and some lost their lives. Survivor's guilt is a real thing, and we felt so grateful to be alive. But Kory's injuries were different, because they weren't severe enough to seek medical treatment, but they were bad enough to cause lasting pain that would take months to heal.

I was much better off than Kory, and a short examination of myself told me how lucky I really was. I had experienced a slight neck injury that limited my mobility, but, once again, I felt it was too minor to seek treatment. No way was I a priority while others needed way more.

After seeing the bruises on each other, we embraced, holding each other close and just breathing as one. We were as close as the night before, when the wind had whipped around us, but now we weren't afraid or trying to survive. We were thanking God for our survival.

We took turns showering and feeling the pure heat and bliss as the water rained over us, cleansing us from such a traumatic night before. It took three rounds of shampoo and almost an entire body bar to scrub the rest of our house and all the debris from our skin and hair. Thankfully, we would have soap refills for tomorrow.

CHAPTER 11

The Lie

Psalms 57:1-2: "Have mercy on me, my God, have mercy on me, for in you I take refuge in the shadow of your wings until the disaster has passed. I cry out to God Most High, to God, who vindicates me. He sends from heaven and saves me."

It is in our weakest moments, when we have fallen to the ground and can no longer stand, that God sends angels to pick us up and comfort us. When we have no strength of our own, we have unlimited strength in Him.

At some point, after all of the chaos had settled and we were left alone in the hotel for the night with our thoughts, we began to feel our injuries. My neck hurt, and I couldn't turn it well, but it was nothing compared to Kory.

After that first hot shower, I helped dress his wounds and inventoried the bruises that covered his back. When the storm hit our home, he wasn't wearing anything but his sweatpants, which meant his bare back absorbed the falling walls, debris, and glass that were headed for my body. This resulted in superficial slashes, bruises of all different colors, and intense soreness that radiated through his body.

One of the worst injuries he sustained was to his left eye. It wasn't anything you would notice by looking at him, but he kept rubbing his eye and described it as if there was something stuck in his eye. This was especially concerning since he'd had Lasik eye surgery done just a few years prior.

Another item of importance was the need for my medication. I'd had my thyroid removed a couple of years prior, due to family history of cancer, an autoimmune disease destroying my poor thyroid, and the silly little nodules that could have been cancer growing in my own neck. Because of removing this vital organ, I was dependent on medication. A day or two without it would leave me feeling sluggish, tired, cold, and in a brain fog, where I could hardly focus on a conversation. It was vital I get my medication. We would have to go to the hospital, where our pharmacy was located, right next to the emergency room.

I'd actually have to go get multiple medications. You see, my thyroid medicine wasn't the only thing I was dependent on. I also took a mild dose of anti-depression medication, and it's quite ironic how I came to be on it.

I am a big believer in mental health counseling, and I saw my own counselor for a few months at a time, as I needed it. Before our lives were turned upside down, I had already needed counseling. A few months prior, I was in a mess with my coworkers, working as a home health physical therapist for a company I had once loved, but had come to dread working every single day. I felt crippling anxiety building daily and a fuse that was inching shorter and shorter, until one day, during a team meeting, I caught fire. I ignited, exploded, and burned at a high level for an ungracious amount of time, to the point where I felt that there was a severe possibility I could be bipolar.

This isn't something to be taken lightly, and I'm not just throwing that word out there to irritate my best friend, who happens to be a counselor and hates it when people use that word nonchalantly.

I truly meant it, though, and my counselor thought it could be a possibility, as well. I was sure I was going to be diagnosed with this mental condition and would require medication to stabilize my highs and lows at the time, which didn't seem to have rhyme or rhythm. So, my counselor sent me to a psychiatrist. This is a fancy word for a medical doctor who can prescribe pills, for the people who need a little something extra. He was private pay, worked an hour away, and had a huge waiting list.

Luckily, I didn't have kids and could afford to prioritize my health, so I called his office up and was promptly placed on a waiting list. *Oh boy,* I thought. This meant months longer dealing with this anxiety and angst. But at least I had a plan and had taken the first steps. I decided to do all that I could to cope in the meantime, which meant avoiding confrontations at the office... Yeah, good luck, sister.

On a particularly busy day, I was driving down a beautiful back road, about to lose cell service, when I got a phone call with a Nashville area code.

"Hello, this is Lauren," I answered, fully expecting Vanderbilt hospital or a doctor's group calling me about one of my patients.

"Hi, Lauren, this is Michelle. And today is your lucky day, because we have an opening for you with the doctor." Her words made my heart leap into my throat.

I pulled over to keep the two bars on my phone from fading away and to jot down the information, including the ungodly amount of money I would need to pay him for an evaluation. That was okay, though: this was the beginning of my road to anxiety management, and I was thankful to have been fit in so quickly!

The day of evaluation came and went, and to my relief and disbelief, I was, in fact, *not* bipolar, just working in a hostile environment without the support I needed and therefore creating an unmanageable rollercoaster of ups and downs, which had resulted in my strained mental state.

The doctor not only gave me a daily medication to help temporarily manage this, but he gave me "in the moment" meds for when I just needed to chill out. When I needed to be calm. When it was all too much and I needed a way to decrease the noise and allow myself the time to process and cope. I thought I would never need those second pills, that my life was pretty chill and stable, aside from this snafu at work. Besides that, I didn't believe in overmedicating and using medicine I didn't absolutely need. Little did I know I would be so grateful for the prescription in facing the upcoming challenges after the storm.

I obviously support medication management for mental conditions. It's vital to address the needs of an individual, including talking about trauma as well as coping with it when it becomes too much. How in the world did God know I would need so much help coping? You see, I started these medications just the month before the storm. One month's medication in my system allowed me to remain levelheaded. It allowed me to cope. It allowed me to feel less out of control, in order to process and live each day. It also gave me access to Ativan and instant relief, when it all became too much. And trust me, it did become too much.

So, long story short, I needed to get my medication prescriptions filled. I could not cope, didn't have a thyroid, and would be developing withdrawal symptoms unless I got those asap. Kory, on the other hand, needed to have his eye looked at. So, for the first time since that night, we split up again. His mom and stepdad drove me to the hospital, where I could go to the pharmacy, and Kory went with his dad and stepmom to have his eye examined.

I knew many of our neighbors had been taken to the local regional hospital, where my husband worked, and where I spent the first year of my physical therapy career a few years prior. Also, because it is a small town, we know everyone.

After going to the pharmacy to request an emergency medication refill, I somehow made it through the hallways of the medical-surgical floor undetected, and went up to my neighbor's room. I felt such a unique pull to see someone familiar, someone who had survived. I have no clue why I didn't wait for Kory, except that my stubborn and independently thinking brain hadn't thought this scenario all the way through before I arrived at his door.

He was surrounded with people, and I was pretty intimidated when every head turned to look at me as I gently knocked on his door. Here I was in jeans that were too big, shoes that needed two pairs of socks to stay on my feet, a bra that hardly did its job, and a shirt that, like the rest, had been borrowed from others, as if I didn't feel enough like an imposter. There I stood while he lay in bed. We had both survived, but he couldn't walk, and I could. I was so glad I could hide beneath the monstrosity of a sweater I was wearing at the time.

Barely looking him in the eye, I stood in the doorway, unable to take another step into his room.

"Lauren, it's so good to see you!" He almost sounded cheerful and relieved, like he was there for a short visit. Not like he didn't have either of his daughters with him or that his wife was in another wing, recovering from her own surgeries and injuries.

"It's good to see you, too. Are you doing okay?" What a silly question. He was casted, bruised, scratched, and looked worse than even Kory did. But. He was alive.

"Yeah, I'm going to be okay. Hey, do you know where my daughter, Madison, is?"

Everyone turned to look at me, expectant and hopeful. I felt two-inches tall and was immediately overwhelmed by so many emotions. *Who in the hell did I think I was? Why did I think I had any right to march down to his room, stand in front of a man who couldn't stand himself, interrupt time with his family, and ask him how he was?*

I should have known it would be hard and that I would be faced with some difficult things, but I'd had no idea he wouldn't know what I knew about his sweet baby girl. I had no idea he wouldn't remember my husband taking her from his arms last night as she lay, angelic, over his shoulder, not breathing, not moving.

"I... I... I'm not sure." I could barely look him in the eye as I lied through my teeth. I felt my throat start to close. I couldn't stand there for long, fixed in the gaze of so many expectant eyes, and keep it together while I fed him the lie. My breathing began to accelerate and my eyes welled up. "I have to go get my medicine and go to Kory, but I'll see you."

I had barely turned to leave before my legs melted into the hard, cold tiles and I collapsed into a nurse's arms. I had never felt so out of control of my body, but it didn't matter. I wanted to die right there, and I felt a thousand knives pierce my heart with the grief I tried so hard to hide from my neighbor.

My shrill, deep, raw screams filled the hallway. I couldn't comprehend how he didn't know about his little girl.

"He doesn't know! He doesn't know where she is!" I sobbed and sobbed into the royal-blue scrubs of another angel.

"Who doesn't know *what?*" Courtney called over some other nurses. They all got me into the nurses' station, and I realized it was Courtney holding me as I sobbed and snotted and collapsed into my emotions. She was a beautiful, blonde nurse who worked with Kory and always helped everyone she could, beyond anyone's expectations. Of course, she did. She was a nurse. I felt safe as I thought back to my neighbor's peaceful and almost happy face, the expectant eyes of his family members, and the sinking feeling I was faced with.

Not only did he not know where his daughter was, he didn't even know she was dead.

Madison. Beautiful Madison. The last memory I had was of her draped peacefully in Kory's arms the other night, as he carried her to safety. I knew she was gone before Kory even told me. I remember her beautiful curls, the bloody spot on her head that I had been sure had caused her premature death, the way she seemed asleep. I would later learn that it wasn't her blood covering her head; it was her dad's blood. What a relief that was. The beautiful angel truly was just asleep, dreaming with our Father above.

Not only did he not know where his daughter was or that she was dead, but while searching for answers from his next-door neighbor, who had appeared out of thin air, and I had lied to him. I didn't have the strength, the bravery, or the plain will to be the one to tell him.

Perhaps he had already known and was on enough medication to mask his sadness. This was the sorry lie I tried to tell myself to ease my own guilt.

How would I ever recover from this moment? How did I think I'd be okay to go down this hall where my neighbors lay, while my own two feet were well enough to walk of their own volition.

How dare I?

CHAPTER 12

All the Gifts

1 Peter 5:10: "And the God of all grace, who called you to his eternal glory in Christ, after you have suffered a little while, will himself restore you and make you strong, firm and steadfast."

God cares for us, and even though we suffer some, He provides for us, giving us gifts and fulfilling our hearts. We must open our eyes to see that the gifts around us come from God as He uses his people to do his work.

We spent many days at the hotel, I think a week in total. It was such a relief to have a home base and somewhere to store what few things we did have.

One of the biggest blessings in my life was my closest friends from college, who lived all over the country. Once they heard of the destruction of our home and belongings, they immediately got to work, using my sister as the point person to help direct them toward my preferences.

Hannah sent me gently used boots from Poshmark and way too many pairs of wool socks. Kat sent me a dozen pairs of underwear and matching raincoats for Kory and me. Her husband, who was stationed in Afghanistan, contacted his friends in Cookeville to provide us support on the ground. My sister helped pick out things and send other essentials, and my mom, fashionista that she is, got on my favorite website, LOFT, and ordered me some jeans, a silk scarf, and a couple of cute tops. It's ironic because looking cute was the last thing on my mind at the time, but I would be so grateful for those things later.

As the days went on, my morning routine changed a bit. It had been reduced to brushing my teeth and hair, and that's about it. There was no makeup, no skin care routine, and no hair styling—not that I did these things every day, but I definitely liked having the option to feel a little extra pretty on certain days.

Losing everything also means you lose a part of your identity as your routines are changed and your possessions no longer exist. I used to live in the identity that I didn't *need* makeup, but when I wanted to, I certainly knew how to glam up a bit, whether it be for work, a dinner party, or just to go grab a drink at the local brewery. When that option is taken away from you, you feel less worthy, less pretty, and less yourself.

Enter Megan and Elisha. Some of our closest friends had wanted to see our faces and hug our necks, so, a few days following our relocation, we decided to meet our friends for dinner. Before this meetup, I wanted to dress up a little but really didn't have the option. That's when Megan and Elisha and I headed to Ulta, a big, new store in town full of hair products, eye shadows, and every lip color imaginable. It was quite classy for our small town.

If you're a glamorous girl and get dressed up every day, or even if you're not, you can appreciate the time it takes to accumulate the gobs of makeup and hair accessories that some girls possess, including me, before the storm. I had makeup my mom had given to me years ago in college that, honestly, probably needed to be thrown out anyway. I had eye shadow of every stage so that Halloween makeup was always covered; we'd get ready at my place. I had perfumes I had hardly ever touched, but that helped to line my bathroom drawers. I had hair products for every possible style and then some, which were for my friends with curly hair, when they came over for a girl's night and we got ready together. Now, I had none of it. When I thought about getting a few things, it was hard to know where to start.

Walking into Ulta should have been exciting and exhilarating; my heart should have been full of anticipation. However, when I walked through the set of glass double doors under the fluorescent lights, I felt overwhelmed and out of place, like an imposter. First, to replace the things that I had would take so much time and so much money, neither of which I was entirely willing to give that night.

After a few deep breaths and getting the attention of one of the sales associates, my friends and I told a small part of my story. The gentleness of the ladies helping me was touching. I followed like a stray puppy from shelf to shelf as they showed me possibilities, made recommendations, and helped me to reestablish a makeup routine that I could enhance or simplify, depending on my needs for the day.

I needed foundation, blush, bronzer, eye shadow, eye liner, mascara, lip gloss, and the proper application tools including a set of brushes. I needed makeup remover to remove my painted face each night, as well. The bag became fuller and fuller; many times, I wanted to just leave the bag and leave the store. Part of me greatly enjoyed the ability to just pick what I wanted and start from scratch, but the other part was greatly overwhelmed and wanted to run out of the building after each corner we rounded.

Finally, we had a base supply of things I felt would suffice for now. I didn't even let myself consider how long it would take to accumulate the rest of the things I wanted to have back. We got in the checkout line, and after a short wait, as I dumped my load out at the register, my two friends took out their credit cards and split the bill. To this day, I get a pit in my stomach about that—not filled with dread, but with gratitude at the thought of my friends taking on that burden to take me shopping and have so much patience as I perused every aisle; and also, to provide that small piece of girliness I craved and needed to begin to recover and to feel like myself again. I was, again, on Cloud Nine as we left the store and headed out to dinner to meet up with our friends and my husband.

We had decided on a local Mexican restaurant, because they had great margaritas and a fine street taco selection. The hugs were tight and long as each of my friends grappled with the thought that Kory and I could, and probably should, be dead. The thought that this meeting might be hard for my friends, as they processed what I'd had days to start processing, never crossed my mind, but I was just grateful everyone was willing to meet on a "school night," as we liked to call it.

We briefly told part of our story, but it was the pictures of our non-existent home and the piles of belongings and splinters we showed them on our phones that really touched people. Our house was a center point of many of our friendships, because, you see, we used to host amazing parties.

One of my favorite parties was our black light party. The back of our house was just a wall of windows, so I had hung white curtains across the full wall to pull for privacy, once the sun set below the horizon. This created the perfect backdrop to create a fluorescent purple glow after we replaced almost every light in the downstairs of our home with a black light. We used a stash of bulbs Kory had kept since his college days, as well. We instructed everyone to wear white and then provided ample highlighters to draw on one another's skin. We had a grand time, eating potluck food, dancing, and just enjoying everyone's company.

We were also known for our awesome Christmas parties. Since we had vaulted ceilings in the living room and a catwalk crossing the second floor from one side of the house to the other, we were able to create a Christmas wonderland. I would string garlands of with lights, ornaments, glitter, and other decorations, after making two to three new strands per year, until we finally had enough to line the front and back of the catwalk, as well as the banister you saw as you entered the front door. I decorated every door with had wreaths and even replaced the paintings on our walls with paintings I had done of Santa or a cute holiday saying, often with slightly inappropriate innuendos, like "I'm on the Naughty List."

I always made a plethora of Christmas cookies from the recipes handed down to me from my mom, and we always had way too much food and drinks. We did a Dirty Santa exchange with wine and liquor, and we cracked open a couple of bottles to share with our guests. Friends came from hours away to stay in one of our three guest rooms and enjoy the festivities with us each year.

All of those decorations, all those memories, all the planning and party-themed platters: they were all gone, demolished into a pile of rubble. When we shared photos with our friends, they mourned the loss with us.

It would be two years before I could go into Hobby Lobby and even consider redecorating or recreating any of the things I had accumulated over time. The usual joy the store brought me would reduce me to tears, if I considered entering in September, when Christmas things were already on shelves, sparkling and calling out to be put on my wall and trees.

After this wonderful yet bittersweet dinner, we headed to the local brewery, the Red Silo, which was owned by some dear friends of ours. Elijah had told us that some locals had purchased T-shirts and pajama bottoms from the brewery's store for us and asked us to come pick them up that evening, if we had time. Little did we know that one of our favorite local hangout spots was also doing a fundraiser for us, collecting cash at the bar from patrons and our friends.

When we got there, we were stunned to find that they had collected a couple of thousand dollars for us. We were shocked and filled with gratitude; my eyes brimmed with tears as we accepted the generous gift. Even though we hadn't found my purse yet and didn't have Kory's wallet, God provided for us at each and every turn.

* * *

At one point, Kory and I had traveled the hour west to see his brother and his family, who had been hit by the same storm cell on the same night we had, a mere forty-five minutes before us. Their neighborhood had been devastated as well; not nearly as badly as ours, but they had homes with half of the roof missing, holes blown through walls, and plenty more areas of "smaller damage."

Their own house had been damaged so much that the roof had to be replaced in the following weeks, along with their air conditioning unit.

When I think back to the fact that both brothers were so affected that night, I think of my poor mother-in-law and what she must have been feeling. She received the first phone call from one brother saying their house had some damage from a tornado, but they were okay. Then, less than two hours later, she heard from me telling her that her other son was barely alive and all of our belongings were gone. That's a moment that hits hard for any mother, but what a gift it was to have them both still living.

Anyway, we went to visit his brother, because we had time, and we needed to go to some bigger stores that our small town didn't have. My sister-in-law, Ashley, took me shopping, because we had a funeral to attend and I didn't own anything black. Also, I didn't own anything nice at that time.

It's a weird feeling to try on dresses for a funeral. I almost wasn't entirely present for that part, but as Ashley and I roamed the aisles, it was hard to feel called to anything in particular, so I settled for a plain, black, knee-length dress with long sleeves. On the way to pay for my dress, I remembered that I didn't have any shoes or a purse, so we stopped by those aisles, too. A small black purse caught my eye, the brand I loved, but it wasn't cheap.

I knew Kory would want me to have something nice after everything we'd been through, so I absentmindedly grabbed it. I also found a pair of black wedges for my tiny size-6 feet, and that was all the shopping I could handle for the day. Finally, we got in line. I was so excited for my purse. I love the small, name-brand bags, and I was lucky enough to spot one in black—how fitting.

After checking out, I took the bulky backpack off my shoulders, set it on the floor, and fished out some money I'd been given. By the time I stood back up, the saleslady was handing my sister-in-law a receipt. Another wave of gratitude mixed with perturbed confusion came over me. I tried to tell Ashley she didn't have to do that, and that she was going through a lot, too.

Ashley is a beautiful, kind, and very soft-spoken woman. When she immediately snapped back at me that she could and *would* do it, I didn't argue back. I accepted the bag of things and followed her back out to the car.

You see, I think people need to feel needed. We all have resources, to some extent, and we all need to feel like we are making a positive impact in the lives of those around us. This was a small but deeply meaningful way people could help us. It was another provision from God.

I realized He was also teaching me to accept the help that I had always yearned to give to others.

CHAPTER 13

The Community

Romans 12:15: "Rejoice with those who rejoice; mourn with those who mourn."

We had no reason to remain in Cookeville, Tennessee. We had no family, no ties, and, after the tornado, no house holding us here. Why, then, did we stay? It was the community. The people who rallied all around us to uplift and support us. That's it.

Cookeville, Tennessee. It's not a tiny town, but it doesn't really show up as a destination, either. Halfway between Nashville and Knoxville, on the plateau, and known more as being a good spot to stop on a road trip, at a crossroads of sorts, it is the home of Tennessee Tech University. When I first moved there, I hated it. There, I said it.

The only reason I accepted the job at the local regional hospital was because Kory had gotten into nursing school on the same day that they had offered me a job; at the time, it had felt like a coincidence and meant to be. Well, we all know how I feel about coincidences now... They don't exist. It is purely a sign from God. The alignment of paths was intentional and led us to be there, so I accepted the grossly low salary offer and signed the lease to our apartment.

Over time, though, I truly grew to love its small-town charm. There were way more young professionals living there than I'd ever imagined, and with the opening of its first brewery, we began to meet more and more like-minded people. After Kory's graduation from nursing school gave us a second income, we began to explore more local restaurants and visited the local winery, eventually becoming members. It was a small enough town that you would be guaranteed to run into someone you knew any night of the week you went out for dinner, but it was large enough that there were always new people to meet.

The other thing that drew us to stay in Cookeville were the amazing outdoor life opportunities. Although I wasn't always known as an outdoors-type girl, I quickly learned that a part of being Kory's wife was either supporting his need to be outdoors or spending way too much time away from him. So I holstered my need for indoor plumbing and a mattress to sleep on, and we began our hiking endeavors.

There were waterfalls and state parks all around us, so we never ran out of places to go. We traded in Kory's one-person sit-in kayak, used to navigate the rapids, for two single-person kayaks we could float down the river on. We bought hiking backpacks that could hold fifty-plus liters of supplies, and I learned what it took to literally carry everything you needed on your back. We often hiked five miles into Virgin Falls, set up camp, and then hiked back out the next morning.

Our love for the town was truly solidified when we built our first home. We lived on the perfect street, with the perfect neighbors, and the perfect group of friends. We'd drink beer, go on hikes, plan trips to see our friends on the other side of the country, and visit my family, who lived at the beach in Florida. Life was good.

Why, then, did we ever consider leaving after the tornado? Really, we did almost leave. There was nothing holding us down. That is, until the town provided everything we needed.

In the aftermath of the tornado, debris was everywhere. Parts of our closet barely moved more than ten feet, while some of our belongings ended up as far as halfway to Knoxville, Tennessee. Yes, from fifty-two miles away, someone called us to say they had one of our tax forms that had blown into their yard. When she asked me if I wanted her to mail it to us, I laughed and told her to shred it.

Anyway, stuff was blown all over the town, and instead of a late-season snow, it was a March Madness of people's belongings.

My mom had meticulously collected important and meaningful documents and awards from my childhood just a few months prior, and she had graciously given the box to me, to be stored in my own attic or spare closet. I went to one of my OB appointments a few weeks after the storm, and they gave me a drawing I had made in the second grade, back when I wasn't a Farmer and still had my maiden name, which someone in the office had found from that very box.

It was crazy to think of my belongings being all over town, but at the time, I didn't even care. They could throw it all away as far as I was concerned. The city, however, took a different stance. I have no idea who thought of it, but they created a storm survivors' hub. The community center was transformed into a rescue center. All the donations of things that had poured in from all over the state and around the nation were gathered, mostly into this location, but the city didn't stop there. They began to ask people to bring in things they found, specifically pictures and knickknacks, and drop them off. Then, a huge group of people began the task of hanging up each individual picture or laying each item out.

They devised a system where those affected could walk through and reclaim their belongings. Every couple of days, Kory and I ventured over, walking the hallways, grabbing our pictures and memories off the walls, and placing them into a bag. It was amazing how our community came together to help us piece our lives back together, one torn picture at a time.

The very first time I went to the donations center, which was in the big auditorium behind there where all the pictures had been hung, I had to sign in and provide my address. Then, I was given a shopping cart and could begin to peruse the aisles of donated items. I remember having so many different feelings.

The first time I went, I was grateful for being able to pick out a pillow that I could call my own, but I felt it was unnecessary to take a blanket when someone else could use it more than I could. I felt sheepish taking soap or Band-Aids and Neosporin, but that was one less trip I'd have to make to CVS in order to treat Kory's wounds. I felt silly taking snacks that I knew I could go to the store and buy, or the feminine products that had been provided, as well. I told one of the volunteers, "No, thank you," when she tried to offer these things to me. When I explained to her why, the look she gave me was heartbreaking.

"Sweetheart, these things are here for people like you."

How do you even process that? I was so concerned about not taking things so that others could have them that I'd failed to realize *I* was the "other people."

Each time I went back, I felt less and less ashamed and more grateful for what our community had done for us. They were there to help us get essentials. They helped us find shelter. They helped us reclaim some of our belongings. They were there to hug me when I found one of my pictures hanging on the wall and shouted, "That's mine!" with tears in my eyes. They cried with me, held me, and gave me hope that there was more that mattered in this world than all of the things we no longer had.

It wasn't just this one place that had set up shop to help those in need. Almost every church received many, many donations, and each facility handled it a little differently. One supportive approach that really stuck with me was at a Baptist church on the north side of town. They had a downtown boutique donate an entire room full of clothes for those who needed them to go through.

My friend mentioned it to me, and I decided I wanted to find some outfits that felt like something I would have bought myself and that would have fit right into my old closet. All I had at the time was ill-fitting jeans and some T-shirts, in addition to the black dress I now owned. I wanted to get some pretty dresses, some leggings, and maybe a nice top.

When we got to the church and checked in, I just stared at the racks of clothes. They filled two rooms. There were purses, shoes, leggings, sweaters, and so many other things you'd find in a cute boutique. Once again, I felt guilty for considering taking some of the pretty things for myself, because I could and probably should have just gone to buy these things myself. However, the kind girls there had to again remind me that these things were here for people like me.

With that thought in mind, I grabbed some items and tried them on, but I just couldn't get into that groove you have to be in to enjoy a girls' shopping trip. Instead, I turned my thoughts to my neighbors, like Jill, who was in the hospital with her recovering baby girl. I thought of Amanda, who was also dealing with injuries and couldn't do things like this for herself.

I estimated the sizes they wore and grabbed a handful of things for them, plus a couple of things for myself that I thought might work. I didn't have much hope for myself, but I had lots of hope for the stash I had for my neighbors. Once again, God used His people to fill the little gaps, and it was such a blessing to have this free shop in the middle of our town, serving those who needed it.

* * *

Frequently, after the storm, Kory and I went back to our lot to go through piles of debris or to sort through some of our things that friends had gathered into a pile, helping us clean up our lot and ease our overwhelm. One day in particular, I remember walking over from Brittney and Jared's, with the intention of digging up some of my plants to save them before they were run over by machinery and trampled by volunteers.

They included my daylilies, which Ms. Marie had given me, my red flowering quince bushes, whose arms stuck out at odd angles, my hydrangea, and my hibiscus bushes with their dinner-plate-sized flowers. I had irises that bloomed in late spring and foxgloves that stood tall with their bell-like blooms hanging down over one another. My hope for a beautiful spring garden had been completely destroyed.

Armed with a shovel and a few disposable pots, I tried to kneel down next to my plants without getting shards of glass in my knees. And then, for what felt like the hundredth time since the storm, I lost it. In one of my most intense breakdowns, I cursed at everything. I was mad at the wind for taking my house. I was mad at the broken glass for making this so hard. I was mad that most of my beautiful flowers and bushes wouldn't make it, and it felt like I was losing a piece of myself. I sobbed and heaved and snotted everywhere.

Becoming frustrated, I threw my shovel and erupted into full-on tantrum tears, while Kory did his best to console me and help dig up the remainder of our plants. Our friend Jared, Brittney's husband, had tagged along, and he tried to turn his back and give us some space, but I didn't even feel embarrassed as my raw emotions ripped through my heart.

That day, digging a few plants out of the dirt really made it real that my house was gone. It pointed out the depth of what I was faced with. I wouldn't be back to weed my gardens that no longer existed or sit on the front porch and admire the blooms on all my bushes. I left most of the plants there that day, which broke my heart, but in reality, I had nowhere to put them and no means to care for them. They'd either be trampled by machinery or the boots of people trying to help us in other ways. The whole situation felt futile.

I don't know how they heard about it, and I don't remember exactly what brought it about, but my favorite nursery in town, Johnson's Nursery, which was owned by our friend from church, heard about our situation. Before I even knew it, they arrived at the house, dug up my salvageable plants, and took them to their own nursery to be cared for. It was such a relief and a huge blessing in my life when I found out, and I gave our friend a call.

He verified that he had saved my plants and was keeping them in the greenhouse, but I could visit them whenever I wanted. As silly as it sounds, I did go visit them. It did my heart so much good to see how many of my beauties were able to bloom later in the year. Some had been pruned back almost to their roots because of the damage they'd sustained, but there was hope for them for next year. The flower doctors had them now, and they would do everything they could to keep my plants alive for the next year, until we had a plan for where we would go next.

As I write this book, my hibiscus bushes have just opened their first purple blooms of the season. The gratitude I have to David for saving my flowers and allowing them to prosper and bloom in their new home is so great, and it has allowed me so much healing.

This community, the stories shared, and the stories that remain untold have all been such a blessing in my life.

CHAPTER 14

The Dress

Deuteronomy 30:3-5: "Your God will restore everything you lost; he'll have compassion on you; he'll come back and pick up the pieces from all the places where you were scattered."

Although not all of our physical possessions were restored, God did restore everything in my heart that I needed to have restored. He gave me peace, helped me see my community and friends at work for me, and even gave me back small, irreplaceable gifts from my old life. He knew what was important and helped to fill my cup.

In the weeks that followed, during our recovery, our community kept scouring the Internet and social media pages, tagging us when our belongings popped or a picture of us appeared and sometimes even documents with our names on them came up. Most of it was neat to get back, but then it would sit in a box or folder, rather useless. Pretty pictures were to be hung in hallways. Torn, smudged pictures that smelled of mildew and that night were put in a box in the back of a closet.

Over time, I became saddened when I thought of something that I knew would never be replaced. One of those somethings was my wedding dress. It was a monstrosity of a gown, with layers and layers of fabric, a cathedral-length train that had bustled up behind me, and gemstones lining the bodice. It had been my dream gown, so, just like every other young bride, it meant a lot to me. The dress had been lost in the storm, along with most of our second story.

Ironically, the delicate canvas picturing my husband and me on our special day, which featured my wedding beautiful gown and had hung above the piano in the foyer of our home, had made it through with a single small tear and some insulation stuck to it that could be wiped off. One of the first pictures we'd taken, along with the damage, on the morning following the storm, was of us holding the huge canvas, standing in front of the destruction.

A picture like that is worth any amount of words. Of course, the photo of us holding our photo spread like wildfire online. People knew I didn't have my dress, but now they knew what it looked like. Miraculously, people found some wedding dresses in piles of the mess. I think three were found in total, and pictures of the stained gowns were posted online and eventually circulated around, but none were mine.

I wasn't hopeful that mine would ever be found. For goodness' sake, my dress had been stored in the same room where we kept our filing cabinet, and some of our tax documents had ended up almost all the way in Knoxville!

One day, I got a phone call from my friend, Liz. She was excited and almost yelled at me, "I think I found your dress!" She told me to check my messages, and sure enough, there was a picture of a young lady holding a blob of white fabric that happened to be my dress. I could never forget the beautiful pattern of rhinestones that adorned its front.

Liz immediately hung up the phone and got to work, tracking down the girl and trying to figure out where she had found that bedraggled fabric. From that point on, Liz made it her mission to track down and save my dress.

The excitement didn't last long. Days went by without hearing much. Every once in a while, Liz would call to ask a question or give me an update, but there was no news on where the dress was.

This poor dress had been a survivor even before this moment after the storm. My parents, as I've mentioned, lived in the panhandle of Florida. Two years prior to our devastating tornado, my parents' home had been hit by Category 5 hurricane Michael. They'd had a great deal of damage to their roof and attic, when a huge old oak tree fell on the house. My dress had been stored in this attic space, and yet, against all odds, it had survived: beautiful, intact, and with pristine white fabric.

My mother had sent it home with us just a few months before the tornado, after our Thanksgiving visit, and we had stored it upstairs. I was planning to preserve it in a shadow box and then donate the skirt to a worthy cause that my mother-in-law had told me about. They take the fabric, cut it up, and make burial gowns for infant babies.

None of this seemed like it would happen, now that my dress was truly lost in the storm.

Kory and I were hanging out one Saturday, drinking beer at our favorite local brewery, when Liz called me, likely for another check in.

"*I found it!*" she screamed into my ear. I was shocked by the volume and the statement, and I couldn't believe it! "I'm on the way to you. Where are you?" she asked, just a little less loud.

When I hung up the phone, I'm sure I had an odd look on my face. Kory immediately asked me what was up. With silent tears of joy, I relayed the good news to him. He was *so* happy to see me so happy to receive a priceless item back.

Liz drove up to the silo, and I ran to her car, where she presented me with my smelly, dirty, layer-upon-layer of fabric that was no longer soft or white, but dirty and covered in mud, insulation, and who knows what else. She immediately snapped my picture and was so excited to share with the whole town what a blessing the day had brought!

She told me she found it at a man's house. He'd said he knew us. It had landed in his yard, and during cleanup and use of heavy equipment, it had been pushed into a pile with other lost belongings, covered in dirt and muck. Ironically, Liz also snapped a picture of him holding up the wedding dress. It was amazing, because we did know this man!

He had been one of the main workers who had helped build our original house. What a coincidence that he would be the one to have my dress. But then again, Cookeville was a town just small enough that something crazy like this could happen.

There were plenty of dry cleaners in town who were cleaning items for free for survivors. We immediately dropped it off with very few expectations. That place had worked many miracles after the storm, but my dress was not one of them.

Because it had sat so long in the muck and debris, it had become permanently stained, and nothing they did worked. I was grateful it smelled better, though, and the sparkling beads were mostly intact.

I wasn't sure what we were going to do with it, but I knew that I was so happy and blessed to have it back.

CHAPTER 15

The Funeral

Matthew 5:4: "Blessed are those who mourn, for they will be comforted."

It is healthy to mourn and lament over things we've lost. Take the time to grieve and to feel all the feelings around each sad moment in life.

With all the joy I felt at being alive and recovering lost items came a deep sadness for those who were not still with us. This grief came in sporadic waves, and each day brought new challenges, including survivor's guilt.

At some point that week, Kory and I made the trip together back to the hospital floor where Kory worked, 5 North. Rounding the corner from the elevators to the unit secretary's desk, someone yelled, "Is that Kory?"

Suddenly, nurses, doctors, aides, and friends from all over flooded to us. We were hugged, kissed, lifted, and prayed over. It was a moment so opposite to what I had experienced just the other day, just down the hallway, with my neighbor. We stood in a circle and received prayers from so many. We cried tears of relief and shared some of our story with the people who were part of Kory's daily work life.

Another day passed, and we knew we had to visit our neighbors Tyler and Amanda, but this time, together. We knew that they knew about their beautiful babies at that point, and we couldn't let fear keep us apart. Not after what we went through together.

Thankfully, they had been moved into the same room on another hall. We walked down the hallway and saw a line of people waiting to see them after their nurse emerged. These people knew, when they saw us, that they would have to wait a little longer, because we needed to see them first.

We needed to know they were okay, and they needed to know that people survived. They needed to know Kory found Madison in Tyler's arms and that Tyler had never let her go. She never touched the ground. From Tyler's to Kory's to Larissa's to Chad's arms. She was always held and loved and cared for. They needed to know that we loved her, too. We walked past everyone else, and it almost felt like Moses parting the Red Sea. There was no questioning us as we gently knocked on the closed door.

When we entered, we saw that they had been given the biggest room on the floor and their beds had been angled together, side by side, facing the window. It wasn't a beautiful view or anything, but it let in the sunshine and allowed them to hold hands across the bed rails, if they chose to do so.

I don't remember our conversation except that it was lighthearted and slightly jovial, as if we were at another small group gathering. Kory had already had a chance to speak to Tyler privately on another day, and they had exchanged more solemn information with each other then. This was not the time for that. At this moment, we were just displaced neighbors, checking in on one another.

There's something you need to know about this amazing family. Tyler was the youth minister at our church. He was a man of God, and Amanda was the epitome of a good Christian wife. She didn't curse, she always smiled, and she raised her girls right.

Madison was an angel. Even before she became a true angel, she was an earth-bound angel. She was courteous, well-behaved, and never acted out, like most young children did. She listened to her mother and, above all, had wisdom beyond her years.

A few weeks after the storm, over a quiet lunch on their parents' land, we ate lunch with Tyler and Amanda, and Amanda told us a beautiful story. A week before the storm, Madison became curious and asked her mother about magnolia trees. What a big word for a little girl! Her mother was confused, because where in the world had Madison heard about that tree? She didn't attend daycare and was hardly ever left unsupervised with the television. What an odd topic.

"Mommy, are there magnolia trees in Tennessee?"

Confused, Amanda told her she didn't know, which was sufficient answer for Madison, and she turned around to continue to enjoy their car ride. They would not understand the beautiful ray of peace that God had saved for them until the moment of Madison's funeral.

I had been to very few funerals in my life, mostly because my family lived a two-day road trip in California, and when great-grandparents died, they never held large services, so we never went. I didn't know what to expect the day it was time for Madison's.

Arriving to the church, I felt numb. This wasn't some grandparent who had lived a long life and to whom we were saying a goodbye, after everyone had expected their passing. No, this was a child. An innocent, well-behaved, beautiful soul of someone whose time with her parents was cut entirely too short. Tyler and Amanda had asked Kory to speak at Madison's funeral, as he had been instrumental in the entire family's rescue and the bond that we had created had been so strong.

Something I had not been aware of most of my life was the traditional views of the church we attended and the church that hosted the funeral. For reasons unknown to me, some tradition I'd balked at and fought my entire time attending was how women were not allowed to address the congregation at the pulpit. I think it has less to do with commands from God and more to do with the traditions experienced in this denomination, more than anything, but that's a topic for another time.

We sat in the front row with our neighbors and held boxes of tissues, waiting for the tears to flow and the noses to drip. It was a great comfort that we were provided a spot to sit and were able to sit together again, displaced neighbors reunited.

When it came time for Kory to read his Bible verse, he stood up, grabbed my hand, and, together, we made our way to the pulpit, ascending the stairs and turning to face the overflowing pews and packed aisleways. Our unity and bond as we stood there meant so much to me, because we had endured that night together, and we would endure this sad moment, just like all the other moments to come, together, as husband and wife.

I didn't know it at the time, but my presence as I walked up the stairs and stood on the stage was a big deal. Even though I didn't speak, I didn't need to. It's amazing when God uses simple actions from His people to represent pivotal moments in a church's history. There we stood, man and woman, equal and linked together by the flesh of our hands.

After we sat and some other people spoke, a line formed to give condolences to Tyler and Amanda. Neither one could stand due to their injuries and each person crouched to give a handshake or a hug and to say words nobody would remember.

As we got to the line, where their parents preceded them in accepting each person, I figured they knew who Kory and I were by the way they looked at us. They said thank you for that night. When we got to our neighbors, I collapsed to my knees and squeezed Amanda's neck. Those couple of seconds burst my heart wide open, and I tried to absorb as much hurt from her heart as I could.

The funeral and burial had all been arranged for Tyler and Amanda by our church and their family, since the couple had been grieving, healing, and homeless, without basic necessities, just like we'd been. After the service, as they were driven up to the cemetery for Madison's graveside burial, the cars pulled up to four beautiful trees that bordered the plot of land that had been donated to the family. The trees had big, waxy leaves and impossibly early blooms that could not be mistaken for anything other than glorious magnolias.

God has answers we will never know until he reveals them to us, but Tyler and Amanda knew that Madison was with God. He had arranged everything, and they were going to be okay. They were going to heal. God would be sure of it.

CHAPTER 16

Temporary Home

Psalms 16:1: "Keep me safe, my God, for in you I take refuge."

God provided shelter to us when we needed it most. We did not have to seek it out, but rather, it found us, and for that, we are eternally grateful.

In the chaos of events following the storm, we had kept the girls with us in the hotel the first night, however, this was not a sustainable plan. We couldn't keep the dogs penned up in a fifth-floor hotel room while we were out all day, slowly putting our lives back together.

I knew the noises of the rooms around them would greatly disturb the girls, and I didn't know if they would bark, growl, or, in their angst, tear up some part of the room. They had never been big chewers, except for that pair of Chacos Kory had left out when Shadow was a puppy and mistook for her chew toy. But we knew how mentally affected by the tornado they had been, just as we had. Who knew how they would behave without us in a strange place with strange noises.

Through the social media grapevine, I heard about a pet boarding place in the town to our north, which was housing displaced animals for free. It was a place we had used for the girls in the past, and it was right next to their vet. This seemed like a good option, but they didn't have a huge yard, and I didn't know how long we would be away from the girls. It was very important to me that they have their space to run and sprint, just like they'd had in their backyard.

There was another local boarder a little closer to "home," wherever that was going to be, and I loved the fact that it was run by a kind, caring woman named Shannon. She had her own special obsession for large dogs and even lived next-door to her business. She had multiple large, fenced-in yards, and the staff there had a special place in their heart for our girls, even before the storm hit.

With some hesitancy and a lot of hope, I sent her a message. At the time, we didn't have much to offer as far as payment, since we hadn't found our wallets and hadn't been gifted all the things we would later receive. I understood if she couldn't take the girls, but she immediately told me, "Bring them to us."

Looking back at the messages brings me to tears. Every time someone was so willing to do absolutely everything they could to help us, which here meant loving and caring for our dogs in a time when we had nothing to give in return. They had kept the girls so much over the years that they were very familiar with their raw diet and peculiar habits. Before I had even begun to think about the things the girls would need, they were provided. They ordered chewing bones, beds, reached out to local places for donated goat's milk and food, and made sure our girls knew they were loved.

After one night in that tiny hotel room with our sweet babies, we drove them up the mountain and dropped them off at their favorite place away from home. Without any hesitation, they bounded into the gate without a second glance back.

It filled my heart with joy and sadness, just as any parent feels when their kid or doggo is so happy to be wherever they are, while not the slightest bit affected by leaving their mom and dad. Shannon assured me they would be well loved. There was not an ounce of doubt in my heart that she was telling the truth.

We had brought some chicken legs, eggs, and Brussels sprouts for the girls to eat. After those ran out, our friends took over. And what a beautiful story that is.

You see, I am *not* a runner. I hate running. I don't even like the game of tag, and I become breathless after approximately twenty seconds doing a light job, largely due to my exercise-induced asthma. Despite all of this, Kory and I had joined a running club.

It wasn't just any running club, though. They were the Red Silo Brewery Running Club. This was a run I could get behind. Every Thursday evening, a large group met at the brewery and groups formed based on abilities, pace, and whether or not you had a stroller. I had begun my journey in the walking group, but with encouragement and lots of tough love, a couple of close friends of mine became instrumental in helping me learn to run a couple of miles at a time.

Slowly, over time, I stretched out my tight calves and hip flexors, improved my breathing technique, and built my endurance so I could do a run/walk combo of three to four miles once a week. It was amazing! It took me months of practice, but each cold beer at the end of Thursday nights and the comradery of my friends made it entirely worth it. We would usually grab to-go dinners from a local restaurant around the corner, choosing between our favorite pizzeria, the local pub, or the new restaurant that had just opened and was always busy. Then, we'd sit outside and enjoy one another's company as the sun set before we all parted ways.

It became something I greatly looked forward to. On the days Kory didn't work, he'd walk/run with me, laughing as I became breathless so quickly while he bounded around me like a gazelle.

On other days, he'd meet us for dinner and a beer after his hospital shift.

After the storm, I vaguely remember seeing some of our running friends around town; they relayed their sorrow for our losses and asked if there was anything they could do for us.

After we dropped the girls off at their own temporary home, I began to stress about how we would be able to feed them. I mentioned this to two of ladies from our running group. I don't remember whom I saw or what I said, exactly, but they made a commitment to help us. So, for the next month, Kory and I rarely had to worry about what the girls were going to eat.

Unfortunately, our misfortune coincided with the beginning of the pandemic. The food shortages scared us and sometimes led us to believe we wouldn't be able to feed Xena and Shadow. But our kind friends took this huge task off our plate and worked directly with Shannon to ensure the Shepherds had everything they needed.

On the girls' second day boarding with Shannon, I received a Facebook message from her. Once again, a stream of tears left my eyes. She had sourced an entire box of the toys they knew the girls loved.

Not only were *we* so genuinely loved, but our girls were, too. That is an indescribable feeling.

* * *

Something we hadn't had to think about much directly following the storm was where we were going to stay. That morning after being torn from our beds, before we even knew to ask for it, our hotel room was booked. We were allowed to extend our stay for an entire week, and to be honest, to this day, I don't even know who picked up the bill. But I hope they know that I'm forever grateful for their generosity and ability to care for us by providing basic needs. I know there are so many others who are not as fortunate to have friends like mine and a church family like ours.

As we arranged to get a rental car, apply for driver's license replacements, and slowly start to buy some necessities, we had to face the fact that there were many displaced families in our town and everyone needed somewhere to go. That group included us.

Immediately following the storm, on our first trip back to the hospital, Kory's boss, Mary, pulled us aside and asked us about our plans for a place to stay. At the time, we'd had no idea where we were going, except on a day-by-day basis. Well, we were as blessed as blessed could be, because she told us of a couple who lived north of town and had an Airbnb that they wanted to donate to a family in need. She had immediately thought of us.

In the moment, we thanked her and told her we'd get back with her, but we weren't keen on the idea of a temporary home and moving from one place to another. A few days passed, and Mary reached out to me again to see what we thought about taking her friends up on this offer. She further explained some details, things I hadn't been able to process the first time we spoke, what with everything going on. She explained to me that it was an entire house, a log cabin on the couple's property, next to a creek. We would be welcome to stay as long as we needed, until we'd had time to figure some things out.

Seeing as we didn't have much of a kitchen and were living on the fifth floor of a hotel, we began seriously to consider the offer. Without much more delay, we decided to accept the cabin, sight unseen. We were just grateful to have a place to call home base, while we figured out our long-term plans.

I remember putting the address into our phone and realizing that this couple lived just half a mile from some of our closest friends, Chris and Summer. That was hopeful, but we also knew that they didn't have cell phone service and relied on a landline for their communication with the outside world, when they weren't in the office of their business.

Heading out to the cabin, we drove farther and farther north and then west, enjoying the beauty of rural Tennessee, which I had grown to love so much. We began to drive along a fenced field with horses, an ass, and a random assortment of other animals. To my astonishment, we turned right and drove over a little bridge above a lovely creek, between two more fences and meadows on either side with more beautiful horses.

It took my breath away when as we drove up a short, winding driveway to a little cabin that stood just fifty yards from the elegant barn that, we soon learned, housed many prize-winning horses.

It was perfect. Small, quaint, and tucked away from the mess of our property, with all the destruction and damage we had to face almost every single day, when we went back for cleanup.

We drove up, entered the code to the back door, and more surprises kept coming. A wood-burning fireplace was the focal point of the living room, with an open-concept kitchen and dining room table, flanked by a bedroom off the kitchen with a Dutch stable door that created the most beautiful ambiance. There were windows filling every wall, letting in the beautiful gray light each morning.

It was funny, though—the sun never fully showed; we lived in constant clouds, each day overcast and slightly damp. But that really was the theme of our life at the time. We knew sunshine was around the corner, but we lived in a dull, faded state of being for that month.

A hallway off the living room brought us to another bedroom, a bathroom with a claw-foot tub, and then a beautiful master suite that had a loft above and a door to the outside. There were dressers, a closet, and even a full-house speaker system, where we could fill the empty space with more cheerful tunes or allow ourselves to remain in a melancholy state, whichever felt more suitable at the moment.

We brought in our few bags and set them down in the spare bedroom, then took in the quaint cottage and relished its perfection. I had recovered one small canvas from our property that I had bought with us. I propped it on the master bedroom dresser, beside the fresh tulips that had been left for us. This was the first picture taken of Kory and me together, years ago, when we met. Although it still had insulation clinging to the back, the front was essentially untouched.

Having it with us added just enough of a personal touch to the space to make me take in a deep breath and start to relax. We would be okay here.

CHAPTER 17

The Road to Get Back on the Road

Isaiah 41:10: "Do not yield to fear, for I am always near. Never turn your gaze away from me, for I am your faithful God. I will infuse you with my strength and help you in every situation. I will hold you firmly, with my victorious right hand."

Even in the moments of flashbacks and difficulties, God is with us and will help us get through hard times.

I had driven two or three times during that first month after the storm, but otherwise had left most of the driving to Kory.

One time, we were driving to church, going down a main street, headed north. We went through an intersection, and in an instant, my head began to spin, and I felt instantly confused. Kory later told me I was screaming things about the night of the storm as I grasped at the door handle of the vehicle and tried to stabilize myself, because it felt like I was spinning and flying all over again.

After ten to fifteen seconds, I came to. Kory had mom-armed me to try to calm me down as he found a spot to pull over. It took a minute to realize what had happened. As I looked at my husband's frightened face, I was afraid to ask him what had happened. Calmly, he tried to explain that I was not present, but was back reliving parts of that night.

Yeah, after that, driving was *not* an option for me for a while.

We both experienced different kinds of flashbacks, but mine seemed to have a greater effect on my physical self and ability to be present in the moment, when the post-traumatic episode hit me. Nighttime was also difficult, and sleep didn't come easy for either of us. Wine, melatonin, and, finally, prescription meds were the paths I used in an attempt to shut out the memories each night. Some methods worked better than others.

The first time I realized Kory was also having flashbacks was one Sunday later that year, at church. We had arrived late, as usual, so we sat toward the back of the spacious auditorium. Partway through the service, we saw one of our elders stand up, looking pale as a ghost, and hurriedly walk to the back toward the doors. He was followed just a second later by his wife, a friend of ours who also worked at the nursing program at the local university. We were twenty feet away as he began to teeter and fall into the doorframe. The crazy part is, my gut told me to get up and help before he began to stagger, but I didn't want to overreact in the moment. Once again, always trust your gut. As he fell, I looked at Kory, and we knew we were going to respond.

Because of our proximity and quick reactions, we were some of the first people who made it to his side. Someone else began to check for his pulse. I remained at his head, staying out of the way until given a task. Too many cooks in the kitchen makes it complicated, so whoever arrives first takes charge—that's what they teach you in CPR class.

I looked over at Kory, who is the ultimate take-charge guy in an emergency, and there he knelt, across our friend's body, but with a look that didn't match the situation we were in. He wasn't confused, and he wasn't afraid, but he was staring at something none of us could see.

He would later tell me that he was seeing back to that night. He saw the trauma and the bodies again, and he felt the adrenaline kick in, as he was expected to respond to the events around him, which included possible fatality. It was all too much. We couldn't stay for much longer after everything subsided.

In the moments following the elder's fall, someone had grabbed an AED and attached the leads. Luckily, as some poor girl was about to prematurely start CPR, the man who lay on the floor was able to belt out, "I'm still alive!"

We all sat back and breathed a sigh of relief. Some guys got him to his feet and helped him into the ambulance someone else had called. This man was not only the husband of one of Kory's coworkers and former instructors, he was also a local doctor in town and the father of a good friend of ours. I felt so blessed that I was able to call our friend and tell him his dad was going to the hospital, but that he looked much better than we had initially thought. He ended up being all right, and for that, we were so grateful.

That episode was hard for Kory. He never really talked about it, and I didn't pressure him to. I knew that these episodes could be confusing, embarrassing to some, and it wasn't a topic of conversation you could force—he would have to tell me in his own time. Because of all the chaos that day, we didn't talk about it for years, not until I started writing this book and began to describe my own flashbacks to him. Only then did I understand that he was just as affected as I was, we just had different ways of expressing it.

So, we weren't sleeping, I didn't have a vehicle, I didn't feel safe to drive. It would take weeks for me to begin to feel comfortable behind the wheel again, and the timing was impeccable, because I had a job to do. God knew I needed a task that was focused on others, in order to get over this fear that had overtaken me.

* * *

For almost a month after the tornado, Kory and I didn't have a vehicle of our own. Both of ours were beyond repair after the storm.

Initially, we relied on the spare vehicle of Kory's awesome cousin, Thomas, until we could get a rental. We had initially qualified for a rental car for each of us, through our insurance policy. However, we got the last car on the lot and they didn't have two to give us. This was perfectly okay, though, because we were rarely apart, and I didn't feel comfortable to drive yet anyway.

We knew we'd have to replace our vehicles and the first priority was getting a truck for Kory. With all the hauling and cleaning of our property, we needed something with a bed we could load things in. We hadn't planned on upgrading Kory's truck for at least five to ten more years, but here we were in a situation where, since we needed a truck, we might as well get the bigger option now, something we could keep long-term and have for when we had kids and needed extra space.

A close friend referred us to a senior manager at the local dealership. On the phone, he asked us what we wanted. We had narrowed it down to a white Ford F-150 or Toyota Tundra. It didn't need to be fancy, and we wanted it slightly used, to avoid the huge expense of a new vehicle.

I kid you not, he told me, "I have one vehicle that matches that description." It was a one-year-old Ford truck without carpet with a roomy cab and plenty of room in the truck bed to do what we needed it to do. We loved that we wouldn't have to deal with carpet, since we used to bring our two German Shepherds everywhere with us. It had 10,000 miles on it and might as well have had our name on it. It was perfect.

We test-drove it once and loved it. But because it was such a big purchase... We told him we would let him know in a couple of days. He promised to hold it for us, since it was under special circumstances.

This was a big-ticket item, but we had our insurance money, we had a definite need for it, and we had to decide if this was the route we would take, because we planned to drive this thing until it fell apart. We went home to sleep on it that night and ask the advice of our parents, but we ended up staying up way too late, as had become our habit. As we lay in the beautiful loft at our little cabin, I was wide awake, having difficulty sleeping, as I listened to Kory snore. We had been through so much, and I knew we needed a vehicle. I also knew how much Kory loved this truck *and* how much he didn't want to ask for something so big, because it felt selfish and unnecessary to him. That night, I made a decision and developed a plan.

The next morning, I got up early, left a note next to Kory telling him I was running some errands, and slipped out the back door. I drove the rental down to the dealership. It wasn't a sunny day, because I don't remember a single sunny day the entire month we lived there, but it wasn't raining, and I had a mission to focus on. Off I went, driving to the southside of town to the dealership.

This was a big moment because I hadn't driven much yet, but I had made the decision to do something for my husband and to take the weight of this big decision off of him. It was the least I could try to do. It was like getting back on a bike. I know that sounds ridiculous, but I was really nervous to get behind the wheel again!

Before I left, I called our truck dealer, letting him know I was on the way, and when I got there, he met me at the side door of the big sales office. I told him the truck was a surprise for Kory, wrote a check, and picked out a specialized Tennessee license tag. (I was very tempted to put my Alma Mata tag from the University of Florida on there, but I thought that may taint the gift just a little.)

The truck was the biggest vehicle I'd ever driven, and I felt like a queen as I drove the twenty minutes back north to our quiet cabin, hoping to get back before Kory woke up. As I rounded the corner and drove over the bridge, around the bend in the road, I laid on the horn in a fun sequence of beeps, hoping to grab Kory's attention without startling the horses too badly. He came walking out the back door and the biggest smile immediately lit up my husband's face.

It was one of the best feelings I could imagine. It grew in the bottom of my stomach all the way up to my heart until I thought I would explode with excitement. I parked the truck at a cool angle, just like those car commercials you see on TV, got out, and tossed the keys over to him.

"Here ya' go!" I was so cool and tried not to fall as I climbed down from the seat.

"What did you do?" he exclaimed, although I could tell he definitely wasn't angry at all. He was like a little boy on Christmas morning.

I couldn't tell you who was happier, he or I. This was not only an amazing surprise, but it represented the first step toward recovery. It was the first big purchase and decision we made, and it felt like a beautiful ray of hope telling us that everything was going to be okay.

CHAPTER 18

Other Big Decisions

Psalms 37:23: "The Lord directs the steps of the godly. He delights in every detail of their lives. Though they stumble, they will never fail, for the Lord holds them by the hand."

We had no idea where we would go or what we would do after the storm, but God guided us, softening our hearts and showing us where He wanted us to be.

Although we had been temporarily cared for and our shelter had been provided, we knew we could not stay in this fairytale cabin forever. The next steps in our housing conundrum included, A, finding a long-term rental, and B, deciding what our long-term plan was after that. Would we go back?

* * *

In the time before the storm, Kory worked not only at the local hospital, but he helped teach clinical rotation for the nursing school at Tennessee Tech University, which was also located in our town. As much as he had hated school when he was studying himself, he was a wonderful instructor. He found it so important to help people learn applicable skills, and he was by far the best trainer for new graduates or new transfers to his unit. It was only natural that he would try to help those still in school, too.

He was no push-over, just ask any of his students, but he made sure to give practical advice, let people learn in a hands-on way, and gave critical feedback so they could learn from mistakes. He was no newbie to failure, and he helped others see, if you didn't get it right the first time, ask for help and keep on trying. He inspired me more and more each time I met one of his students who could not stop singing his praises.

After a couple of semesters helping to teach in his program, he became close with the other instructors, which was completely part of God's plan, because after the storm, when we went to visit the school and the other faculty, we were once again bombarded with opportunities.

One instructor in particular, Rachel, told us about her completely vacant home, because she was living with her parents at the time while she raised her two kiddos as a single mom and had a more than full-time career. She had a beautiful, two-story home not far from our church, and the best part was she had a fenced in yard! We would be able to bring our girls home with us!

Not only did she have a fenced-in yard, her home was fully furnished, as she lived with her parents. She had left all of her couches, beds, dressers, pots and pans, dishes, and anything else you could possibly need to live comfortably. For a couple who had just lost everything, we could not possibly have thought to ask for anything more.

Except, there was more. We didn't have to be concerned with the girls being in the home, because she had had a large dog with anxiety who had scratched at the back door and left marks on her floors, so our girls' nails and any potential damage was moot.

We arranged a time to go over and check the place out. As we pulled up, we realized that this home was on a cul-de-sac in a quiet neighborhood, just like ours had been. The beautiful brick home was at the end of the street, and although the backyard wasn't as big as ours had been, it was plenty big for two Shepherds to chase ball after ball and stretch their legs. She hadn't been kidding: her kitchen remained intact, and she even had an extra fridge in the garage for us to store the dog's raw food in, too!

That day, God provided answers to two prayers. For us, we had found shelter, and for her, she found a way to cover the mortgage for a house she was not occupying. We created a rental agreement, sent it to our insurance company, and they quickly approved our new living arrangements.

Another one of God's blessings was to ensure we had more than adequate insurance coverage. We were blessed that our rental would be covered for an entire year, while we tried to figure out what in the world we were going to do permanently.

Before we moved in, Rachel and her parents completed a deep clean on the home. They scrubbed the fridge, went through the junk drawer, cleaned out the pantry, leaving essentials for us, and made sure the space was something we could really enjoy.

The following week, we dedicated ourselves to creating a space that felt like home, as best as we could. We replaced our brand-new king-sized bed that had, ironically, landed a few streets over after the storm and was featured in a local country artist's music video, placing it in the master bedroom upstairs. We took down, with Rachel's permission, the photos of her kids and replaced them with salvaged photos from our home and a new piece my friend Kinsey had painted of our old home.

We had recovered one of our metal signs with a cursive "F" and hung that, too. I purchased organizing boxes off Amazon and acquired a new blanket from the community center donation pile that would go in there, along with dog toys. We got couch covers for the couches, as Rachel had cats and Kory was severely allergic and couldn't sit on the couches without sneezing up a storm. I even splurged and bought an outdoor umbrella and sectional, so I could enjoy the beautiful back patio with the stone fireplace.

Finally, it was move-in day. Despite the new advice to stay away from other people and quarantine, due to the slow beginnings of the pandemic, our friends all showed up. Sixteen of them, to be exact. We cleaned the blinds, mopped floors, and made a trip to the grocery store. We moved in our bed, organized the closet, and repaired the fence, so the girls couldn't finagle their way out to chase the deer nearby. We removed curtains, deep cleaned rugs, and by the end of the day, we were all exhausted and ready for a beer and pizza. Even though we really didn't have much stuff, we could not have done all of the work we did that day without the support from our lovely friends.

The next day, we picked up the girls from their retreat and tentatively drove back to the new house, all their new toys, dog beds, and bones in tow. The girls were instantly excited, and they began exploring the entire home. The wooden staircase was something they'd have to get used to, but it sure didn't slow them down. I think their favorite part was the storm door that allowed us to open the front door so they could see to the outside and protect the front yard from the terror of squirrels and rabbits that came to munch on the foliage.

Kory and I discovered that the double-stacked windows in the living room, directly in front of the wooden deck, would open from the bottom. We realized it doubled as the perfect doggie door, allowing the girls to come in and out with a swift jump, when we had it open. They also made the living room their "base," as they played tag around the unused trampoline and playset in the backyard. It brought us so much joy to see them chase each other and really start to settle into this new life we were creating.

I got back to cooking and quickly learned the location of all the accessories in the kitchen. We did some reorganizing to make it feel like our own, and I made a list of the herbs and spices I'd need to make our favorite dishes.

Once we settled into our new home, we began to think of our long-term plans. Would we move to be closer to my parents in Florida? Or go to Chattanooga, to be with Kory's parents? Would we buy that land in South Carolina next to our friends, which we'd been dreaming about for a year? Would we buy property in town or right outside of town and stay in this place we'd grown to love? We could always move closer to the center of town and get an older house to fix up and make our own.

When the possibilities are endless, the potential can be paralyzing. We continued to do research online and explore our options without a set deadline in mind. The other important thing to remember was the dozens of other families who were displaced from their homes and also looking to purchase land or homes in the area or even just rent. The options were slim. Sure, we had a rental home, but that was just temporary.

* * *

If you had asked me within the first month after surviving if we would ever go back to that street, in some attempt to recreate our lives and rebuild a one-of-a-kind neighborhood, I would have rolled my eyes and thought you were insensitive. Because who could ever go back after everything that had happened that night? Nothing but pure destruction remained where happy families and beautiful homes used to stand. There were no trees left, driveways were cracked and unusable, and the glass and debris that littered the lawns of our homes was never-ending.

Every time we thought about driving back down that street, once it was finally cleared out enough to do so, I was filled with dread, because there was so much to do and clean-up. At first, we had no idea what the steps were to begin the clean-up process, but we later learned we didn't have to do it alone.

I really wanted to buy land and have horses, so our search began there. We ended up finding an unlisted property that we'd heard about through the grapevine of people at church. We prepared to make an offer to the man who owned it, without his even knowing we were interested. It had a creek, a plateau, and a wooded area—literally everything we had dreamed of, and it was only a fifteen-minute drive from the hospital.

During this whole time, I was adamant that we would not return to our original neighborhood. I knew Chad and Jill wouldn't go back, Luke and Amy would move to a different part of town, and Tyler and Amanda could never go back, either. We were losing our small group, our neighbors, our friends, and the best thing about our neighborhood. How in the world would we ever be able to go back and have half of what we started with?

Late one night, after playing online games with my college girlfriends and husbands, and after sharing a bottle of wine together, Kory had the courage to ask me, "What if we went back?"

I immediately balked at the idea, flooded with images from that dreaded night. The piles of rubble, the screaming of my neighbors, the loss of everything we had loved. How could he even suggest something that crazy?

"Absolutely not," was my instinctual retort, however I wanted to hear what brought this crazy thought to his mind.

Although his specific reasons escape me, they weren't the important part. The most important thing to me was how he began to build a story of hope in my heart. Of course, things would never be the same, and our street would likely be filled with different people, but we could rebuild the house we really wanted, have our land back, and bring the girls home.

We slowly learned that Eric, Eric, and VanEric (yes, three Erics representing three separate families) would all be returning. Tony was going back, and of course, Brittney and Jared were staying, since their home was essentially undamaged, although it was than a quarter of a mile from ours. If they were all rebuilding and going back, why couldn't we?

We wondered what people who weren't going back were going to do with their lots. I'm sure they would sell them, and that made me nervous, because it meant builders we didn't know coming in and selling to people we didn't know, either. It was a scary thought until Kory had a brilliant idea to reach out to our next-door neighbors and see if we could buy their lot right next to ours. With the extra space, we could build in the middle, and in doing so, not only would we create the best backyard for our girls, but we would delete that address from our town forever. Nobody would ever live at the address where their beautiful angel had lived.

Immediately, they agreed to sell to us. And just like that, without a whole lot of thought from either one of us, God had put us back where He wanted us. Once this became an option, I don't remember considering anything else. Why would we? A local lawyer from our church arranged the paperwork, and we signed papers, wrote a check, and just like that, we had an acre.

In case you didn't know, you can't just buy two lots next to each other and expect it all to be okay. You have to have them surveyed and combined, which can get pricey, but once again, God made a way where He wanted us to go.

Larry, our previous builder, had made some phone calls and told us of a local surveyor who wanted to do it for us for free. Once again, I was speechless, grateful, and it felt right making this next move.

* * *

Now that we had decided what we were going to do, we needed to prep our land and make it livable again. The winds from the storm had scattered debris everywhere, and although the big things had been removed, there was still glass, pieces of siding, and remnants of our previous life half buried in the dirt. Not only that, we still had all the concrete from the beginning stages required to build a house.

It would require some heavy equipment, but the first large task was to remove old footers and old driveways that were no longer usable, since they had been cracked by the heavy machinery during the process of looking for survivors. We had been given a small stipend from our insurance company to cover part of this cost, but we learned it would not be nearly enough, especially with the two plots of land we were now responsible for clearing.

Once again, a blessing from God would soon find its way to us. A volunteer organization from out of state contacted us and told us they were working with families who were staying and possibly rebuilding, to help bring in the necessary equipment to dig up the concrete buried in the ground. They would help move it to the edge of the road, and the city was organizing huge pickup trucks to come remove the unwanted materials. We were thrilled, shocked, and so thankful that someone else was coming to help us solve yet another problem we didn't even know we had until it was already addressed.

The equipment and manpower came. They removed the concrete, and we were left with gravel that could be repurposed for the driveway and foundation of our new home.

When we came back to the lots, we decided we wanted to commemorate the moment of starting fresh, so we took pictures.

Some of the first pictures of us smiling again, holding our sign reading "Putnam Strong." We were so strong, but it wasn't by ourselves. It was because of the whole community.

The next round of clean-up came. The daunting task was to remove as much of the little things as we could. If we wanted our future kids to be able to play barefoot in the backyard, we'd have to pick up every tiny shard of glass we could.

It was a hot summer day. After advertising with our church, close friends, and Facebook friends, we gathered with trash bags, gloves, and an assignment to just clean. That morning, we were once again amazed at the turn out of our community. At least fifty people from around the neighborhood and town showed up to lend a hand. For hours, we spread out across the acre, although it seemed like a football field at the time, stooped over, and just picked things up.

We filled trash bag after trash bag and wheelbarrow after wheelbarrow with pieces of our old house and other houses. It was so important for Kory and me to see the support and love that was pouring into our lives, but it was also important for friends and family to see what was left. There were bent pieces of siding, remnants of furniture, scraps of tile and granite countertops. It was so humbling to see what these winds could do, absolutely destroying granite and marble stones into a hundred pieces, yet leaving a soft and breakable human in one piece—mostly.

For lunch, our friend brought us pizza that she refused to let me buy, and we all ate in whatever shade we could find. You see, most of the trees were gone, and for the first time I can remember since the tornado hit, it was a hot, sunny day.

CHAPTER 19

Permanent Home

Matthew 7:24-25: "Therefore everyone who hears these words of mine and puts them into practice is like a wise man who built his house on the rock. The rain came down, the streams rose, and the winds blew and beat against that house; yet it did not fall, because it had its foundation on the rock."

Deciding to rebuild was a decision led by God. We did our best to follow His plan to create the best possible life in accordance with His will.

This is where the fun begins. The design. Think of your or your wife's favorite HGTV show, where Joanna and her goofy husband create a beautiful living space with light colors, natural wood, and touches of homeyness. The options were endless.

The first step was to pick a layout. I knew I didn't want a second floor again, because if we'd had babies during that storm, we wouldn't have had time to get to them, and everyone would have perished. That wasn't something I could wrap my head around. Since we had an acre now, we could have a longer home and not put our future kids upstairs.

After what felt like hours upon hours of never-ending searches, it was Kory who found the floor plan we went with. I was easily overwhelmed at all the options and could get lost in designing some dream home that was completely impractical. Then, he would bring me back to earth by sending me different options of layouts that were similar to our last one, since we loved the downstairs so much. One day, he sent a layout that really stood out to me. The picture of the front design immediately caught my eye. It was perfect.

Our first house was the ideal shade of blue. I'd always dreamed of having a blue house in a deep, rich color that wasn't too bold but had just enough hue to contrast with the beautiful sunset skies. Our home had thick, white trim, a light wood front porch, and lots of windows. It stood high in the sky, with vaulted living room ceilings and skylights; we never wanted for more sunlight streaming through in the mornings.

I couldn't bring myself to build another blue house, though. The memories were too much for me, and I knew I'd never be able to move on from that night, if I drove up to the same blue siding every day. The next best option, and one I'd never really considered before, was white. Yes. Your typical farmhouse, with beautiful wood beams in the front, a large front porch, and the ability to sit on a rocking chair and enjoy the sunset as it disappeared over the edge of Hensley Drive. I'd never really considered white before, because Chad and Jill's white house with the red front door was one of a kind, and we couldn't have two white houses almost side by side. But, now that those old houses were gone, the slate was clean, and the possibilities were endless. I knew I wanted my white farmhouse to have black trim, dark windows, and an even bigger porch than the last time.

This house was an absolute dream. We called it the twenty-year plan sped up. It was something we would have dreamed of owning in twenty years, after we had saved and worn out the first house, but our plans were unexpectedly expedited. If you've ever built a house before, you know how you can customize absolutely everything.

You also know that, as soon as it's done, there is instant regret about things you didn't add or rooms you should have altered or things you would have done differently. Well, here we were—our second chance to redo things and make it the way we really wanted it.

Those things included a walk-in pantry, a laundry room attached to the master bedroom, a soaker tub, and a glass door to my walk-in shower, so I wouldn't get my closet floors all wet and end up installing a crappy curtain anyway. I could get a double oven, create a coffee bar, and have my dream dining room. I wanted wood beams on the ceiling of the living room and a garage with extra space next to the two cars for our storm shelter, which would be an absolute necessity for us to go back to living on that road. We were beyond blessed with the first home, because we had put so much sweat equity into it. Now that we were both working, we were able to afford to get things we wouldn't have dreamed of putting in the first house.

* * *

As we planned the design, hired a contractor, and got started, we periodically visited the lot. After the old driveways to our house and the one next to us were removed from the property, we would sit on the gravel that remained and dream of the next home, where we would hopefully raise a family. Each visit led to new and beautiful discoveries, little gifts from God that showed us we were on the right path.

The first one was the most beautiful and delicate blue egg that lay at the foot of our first maple tree. After we built our first home, we decided to start planting trees that would one day hold a tire swing for our kids and provide shade for the girls after they played ball all afternoon. I love the colors of maple trees, so we decided on an October glory that would change leaves into beautiful shades of oranges, reds, and yellows, before falling to the ground and starting over each year. We dug the hole through the clay by hand, rolled the root ball into the ground, and covered it back up, watering it diligently that whole first summer.

That sturdy tree was only a year old before it endured the worst storm of its life, too, but, just like us, it survived. It was tattered, splintered, and had lost some limbs, but the base stood firm. It was able to recover from the split that sliced its trunk down the middle. We called it the tree's scar and named the tree "Old Faithful." He was the original, and he represented strength.

Anyway, during one of our cleanup sessions, when the entire neighborhood was still in shambles, we discovered this tiny little egg at the base of Old Faithful, not in any nest and without any protection. It was a symbol of hope that, throughout this mess and destruction, beautiful and delicate things could still exist.

It lasted for a few visits until someone handled it at a clean-up and accidentally broke it. They broke a piece of my heart along with it. I was so sad to lose that little egg.

* * *

As the house was being built, we liked to visit it in different stages and just hang out. Sometimes, we'd bring dinner or a couple of beers and just spend time, dreaming of what we were rebuilding.

During one of our picnics at the property, before the gravel had been cleared and the new foundation poured, we were walking around, picking through new debris that had risen to the surface after the latest rain, when I gasped! Quickly, Kory ran over to me, ready to hold me in preparation for another meltdown. I did indeed start crying, not believing my eyes.

The first year after we moved into the house, I'd tried to get into gardening. I loved pulling up weeds, nourishing flowers, and watching things blossom all summer. Despite my inability to keep anything inside the house alive, I had a true green thumb for the outside elements, and I was good at arranging flowers and plants into a beautiful, captivating landscapes.

Before starting my endeavors, I met the most wonderful lady, Ms. Marie. We would take long walks in her garden, which was full of every flower and bloom imaginable. She taught me the names of each plant, when they bloomed, how much sun they preferred, and how to create new plants from existing ones. She was a wonderful woman and got me started on my very first garden. I showed up to her house one day, and she had almost thirty cuts of different flowers ready for me, along with a cute, bushy plant that was potted in its own container.

"It's a limelight hydrangea," she informed me with a wide smile and hunched posture, leaning on her cane. She knew how much I loved hydrangeas, and her bushes grew to be over eight feet tall each year, gracing the back of her property with huge, white blooms, so she had ordered me my very own. It would yield beautiful, white flowers that faded into lime green as summer wore on. The gesture brought me to tears. I was so grateful for the lovely plant and put it front and center in my front garden, between the garage and front steps, where it overtook that side of the porch for two springs.

In front of it, I added the hastas, day lilies, and irises she gave me, as well.

Amongst all the perennial blooms, I sprinkled poppy seeds that were supposed to bring bright-red flowers in a couple of months, but to my dismay, only one ever came blossomed. It had the smallest red bloom that lasted but a day or two before fading away. This was the first time I hadn't been successful at growing something in my garden, but I'd tried to forget about the poppies and move on with cultivating other wonderful blooms.

So, on that day, during our picnic, walking through the gravel, it was absolutely not even possible that, through the rubble, dozens of poppies had sprung up in the spot where my small garden had stood, before being destroyed. The tall, majestic stems held unfolded petals, still safe in their cocoon. On our next visit, they began to open their beautiful, red petals, and God continued to bless the land we lived on.

* * *

After deciding to rebuild, we immediately sought prayers from our church family and friends, helping to ensure this was the right decision for us.

After significant thought, Kory decided he wanted to stake our property. Now, I'm going to be honest, the first time I heard about this, I pictured a ritual involving garlic and the warding off of vampires. That's seriously what this reminded me of. However, after seeing God show up all throughout my life, helping me to heal and rebuild, I knew it was something we had to do, too.

One day, as the sun set behind Hensley Drive, twenty to thirty people gathered on our newly united piece of property and offered up words of prayer. We walked to all four corners of the lot and hammered in posts, dedicating our ground to God and forbidding any and all other non-Holy spirits from ever affecting our property again. It was truly cathartic. To this day, whenever I'm worried about ailments affecting our baby's health, negative emotions I may have let creep in, or days of difficulties with my faith, I remember back to this day and that I live on Holy Land, dedicated to God and His will.

Following suit with our theme of blessings, the frame of our house went up quickly. It became easier and easier to envision where our living room ended and the dining room began, or how incredibly big my new closet would be. As each piece went up, we decided we would begin blessing the home just like we did the lot.

We invited friends and family to come over and write scripture verses on our frame, the subfloors, and anywhere they could think to get a Sharpie. For people who weren't religious, we invited them to write things that inspired hope, putting a piece of themselves in our home. Our family who lived out of town sent us verses they would like written in their honor, with notes on where we should put them. One of my favorites was from my sister, who requested an inside joke between her, my dad, and myself about a particular *South Park* episode, placed on the floor of my closet. You better believe I wrote it down, giggling the whole time.

Kory blessed the doorways of our house with Joshua 24:14: "As for me and my house, we will serve the Lord."

Those words were repeated in my head each and every time we walked into the house and helped guide my decisions, hoping they were right and in God's plan for me.

My personal verse, one I had prayed and prayed for so many years, was 1 Samuel 1:27: "For this child I have prayed." We had struggled with infertility for years, and as I was in my thirties, I felt like my dream was drifting further and further away.

I wrote it in the northwest bedroom, hoping that the beautiful window there would eventually allow in so much sunlight, it would eventually hold the baby of my dreams.

CHAPTER 20

The Child I Can't Seem to Have

1 Samuel 1:27-28: "I prayed for this child and the Lord has granted me what I asked of Him. So now, I give him to the Lord. For his whole life he will be given over to the Lord."

So often, we pray for things and can't imagine our life without those things. We beg and beg God to fulfill our prayers. But we forget to stop and consider that we would not be able to handle these things at this moment in time. This lesson is only learned after the trial is over and we can look back and thank God for sticking to His plan and not ours.

Since I was a small child, I have dreamed of being a mom and a wife. When I was three, I wanted to be a bride for Halloween, or so my mother tells me. I wore a huge, poofy, white dress with a veil and carried a white basket. That veil was again used at my bachelorette party many decades later, as my first dream became fulfilled. I would carry my baby dolls around, feeding them when my mother fed my little sister after she was born.

I was a natural nurturer and always helped care for younger cousins and friends, always wanting to hold the babies. As I grew up and pursued my dreams, I got older and older. And although I got married at an age many years older than my parents had, I thought I'd still have plenty of time to make my own family a reality.

My graduate school was followed by Kory's nursing school and that was followed by building a house and spending time together as working adults. DINKS (dual income, no kids) was a title we sported proudly, enjoying all the freedoms it allowed, but on the inside, I longed for the sweet baby who would call me Momma.

After years of dropping the goalie, throwing inhibition to the wind, and just seeing what happens, we were still unsuccessful. There were numerous months when I just knew that this was it, we were pregnant, and our lives were about to change. Then, one week later, I'd continue on with a broken heart, a frustrated husband, and no baby growing in my belly. At first, it wasn't a big deal. I knew the statistics were that it could take one year for ninety percent of couples to conceive, but there we were, without a baby, over a year in.

It didn't matter that we lived in an apartment, that I drove a two-door hatchback sports car, or that we didn't have a baby's room available. People with much different circumstances made it work all the time, and I knew we would, too.

Then there was one month when I was late for my period by two days, and I just knew: this was it. I was excited but didn't want to worry Kory yet again, until I knew for sure. I couldn't help myself, though, and took a pregnancy test, knowing it was way too early for anything to show up. As if reading my mind, it showed just that: nothing. I wasn't ready to give up hope on another month, though, so I kept my fire going. The next night, I woke up in the middle of the night with the worst headache I'd ever experienced. The piercing pain made me cry out, waking up Kory next to me.

His concern was all over his face, and we moved into the living room, placing me in the recliner, where he tried to comfort me while still rubbing the sleep out of his eyes. The piercing pain only worsened. We called his mom, who was also a nurse, at 2 a.m., wondering if this was emergency-room worthy. By the way, if you're ever wondering if you should go to the ER, don't call a nurse. The answer is always no, which is why I knew calling my own nurse mom would be pointless, as well.

We waited the night out, and neither one of us got much sleep. But at some point, we both passed out. I awoke to a minor headache and relief that the pain had subsided. Relief that I thanked God for until later, when I realized I was, indeed, not pregnant again. This time, though, it was different. I might have been pregnant, because, though I'll spare you the details, the pain of an unconfirmed loss was enough to make me an emotional wreck for the rest of the day.

After that month, I stopped hoping for a while. The loss was too much for me. Because it wasn't ever confirmed, in many people's eyes, it "didn't count" and would never be acknowledged, which made it even harder for me to face. What if my body really couldn't make me a mother? It was a thought I pushed from my mind, but I would occasionally revisit it from time to time.

At my next annual appointment, I discussed our inability to conceive with our doctor, and we talked about different options and diagnoses. At the time, surgery was too far-fetched, so we decided to try some lifestyle changes and increase our efforts before going to extremes.

In the meantime, we had begun building the house and become distracted with our furry children. Thoughts would frequently come to my mind about fostering and adoption, but those seemed difficult. I watched friends and some of our family go through the chaotic process of heartbreak after heartbreak, before they got their miracle children.

Another year went by, and when no children grew in my belly, we decided it was time to move forward with medical intervention.

That first step was to address my endometriosis, and the only way to do that was surgical intervention. I wasn't afraid of surgery; I'd had my thyroid removed in the past and knew how tough anesthesia could be for me. If it led to the discovery of something that wasn't working, though, I knew it'd be worth it.

A whole lot of bloating and some healing incisions later, we learned that, thankfully, none of my baby parts were affected. My, this was a blessing and also such a curse to hear. Now, we had even fewer answers and more interventions to endure. After that, we had another, "less invasive" procedure, but if you ask me, it was worse. I passed that test with flying colors, too, and all I could think was that a baby wasn't in my cards.

I began to push back against nature and God's unwillingness to bless me with a baby and started to convince myself I didn't want a baby. I would be just fine, taking extravagant vacations, adding a pool, and spending the weekends on the lake, without worrying about a nap schedule. I became more and more vocal with my decision. My parents, even my father, tried to convince me that I did indeed want a baby for all the reasons you can imagine. Didn't they understand I was just protecting my heart? It was easier if the decision to not have a child was mine, rather than one my body made for me.

Time continued to go by with less and less baby talk and hopes of starting a family. Later, when we were hit by the tornado, so many of our friends had babies who were severely injured and some even killed. Kory and I could hardly discuss it, but we knew, if we'd had children, they, too, may have been killed, along with us both, because they would have been on the second floor of that beautiful blue home. The thought was sobering. We realized that, after all this time, God wasn't withholding children from us. He was protecting our beautiful, unborn babies. Our greatest despair and distress were, in all reality, such a blessing.

After that moment, we realized we were not ready for children, because we had more work to do for God. We refocused, helping the community and helping ourselves to recover.

Time kept going by, though, and at our next annual appointment, we requested an appointment with a specialist to see what was the root cause of our inability to conceive. The waiting list was long, so we waited and waited and, eventually, forgot about it again, which would prove to be to our benefit and exactly what God wanted for His plan.

CHAPTER 21

You Can't Outgive God

Hebrews 13:16: "Don't forget to do good and to share what you have with those in need, for such sacrifices are very pleasing to Him."

When my resources are plentiful, I long to share them with others. When my resources are limited, God blesses others so that they may do the same for me. Each time we tried to give away what was given to us, God gave us even more.

After the tornado, I was very involved in the reconstruction of the lives of others. Perhaps I felt, if I could help other people get their lives in order and provide them with just small comforts, then I would be making a difference.

Since I wasn't ready to go back to work yet, I had a lot of spare time on my hands. Many hours of my day were spent dealing with insurance claims, working with our contractor, researching what we would put in the new house, and just daydreaming.

The cottage we stayed in for a month, graciously given to us free of charge, allowed us to wake up to the crisp March air every morning, hear the running water in the nearby creek, start a fire in the wood-burning fireplace, and sip coffee as we snuggled under blankets. The damp days seemed to linger, so I got really good at starting fires. I began to make challenges for myself, seeing which way organizing the logs burned most efficiently, gave off the most heat, lit up the quickest, and brought the most beautiful display of dancing flames.

Something else I did to pass the time was contact our neighbors. Some were still in hospitals; we visited those who were local. Some were in rentals around town, and some were able to go back to their homes, due to minor damage. One family I took a special interest in used to live a couple of houses down from us. The mother and father were severely injured, but their three older children were mostly unhurt. They were living with a coworker after both had healed from surgeries, and they were prepared to find a place to settle.

When Kory and I found out where they were staying, we immediately loaded the truck with water, Powerade, and snacks from the police department's donation center, and we were off to the other side of town. By the way, when you live in rural Tennessee, the other side of town is only ten to fifteen minutes away. Anywho! I tentatively knocked on their door, and when the woman answered, I felt like a child again, so unsure of what I was doing.

I pushed that away and asked if our neighbors were staying there, as we had shown up unannounced. She cautiously said yes, and I explained how we had also survived the tornado and lived three houses down.

She led us back down through the kitchen and around the corner to a hallway, where I nervously poked my head around the corner and knocked. The sweetest voice in the world told us to come in. The look on Joyce's face when she saw us made all my worries disappear.

Joyce was *so* glad to see us, and although she couldn't stand to greet us, she gave such a warm hug. They told us of their plans to move to a house a little ways away, and we told her about the goodies we had brought.

After some small talk and asking her kiddos what they were missing, I began my quest. I created an Amazon list and started to help fill their needs. Neither one of them could drive, their eldest son was not quite of driving age, and they were housebound in every sense.

I have always been fairly active on social media and had an inbox *full* of people just begging to help in some way. People from near and far, plus people from different periods of my life had all reached out. I finally had a way they could help. I created the Amazon wish list, posted it, and watched as everything was purchased off the list over the course of that day. Books the kids had requested, blankets, a new stethoscope for Joyce, as she was a nursing student, a set of knives, Tupperware, kitchen accessories and coffee mugs. We even got a specialized Tennessee Tech mug for Joseph, too.

Handpicking things for their kitchen was cathartic and so therapeutic for my soul, because I could dream about the new, but not have to worry about my immediate or future needs, which I had become good at ignoring. Towels, sheets, bedspreads, silverware sets, bathrobes for each kid—I really don't know how I even came up with half of the list, to be honest.

It. All. Got. Purchased. Seeing the boxes grow around the hallways each time we went to visit was so beautiful. But I think my favorite part was when they told us they were ready to move the following week. Although they didn't have nearly the amount of things that someone who had lived with three children for a decade should have, they were unable to walk and so unable to get things to their new home.

Here. Here, we could help again. Kory and I readily volunteered not only our truck, but our physical ability to move all their boxes to the new home. Their eldest son came with us, and we took numerous truckloads full of Amazon boxes, donated food and clothes, and a few salvaged items. It was busy work, but it meant something to someone and continued to take our mind off of our own problems.

Next on my list of people to start helping build back their lives was Laura. She had been in rehab in another city, away from family and friends, and she could have no visitors due to the new pandemic (which was really just an afterthought for most of us). Not only was she rehabilitating herself physically, she was suffering mentally and emotionally, as she worked through all her trauma on her own. My heart went out to her: I couldn't even imagine everything she was going through. I had two working legs and a broken heart, so I had no idea how being completely physically broken would be infinitely worse, but I felt for her.

Though she lived far away, her daughter was involved in some of her mother's care, so I reached out, and we began another Amazon list. Laura was especially fun to create for, because she had no idea we were organizing this *and* she was such a fun, energetic soul with an above-average Rae Dunn obsession, so creating her list was super-fun.

Her list included wine glasses, pink accessories, and a grilling set for her husband. I even got over myself and ordered her alma mater's throw blanket, despite it being a rival of my own undergrad college. We ordered picture frames, a toaster, hot-pink oven mitts, a tool box, an Instant Pot, and bakeware. I posted the list, then the joy of my day started with checking on what had been purchased.

I remember the day she got her first delivery. She had been in her new rental home for just a short time, after returning home from rehab and hospital stays, and she had no idea what all these boxes were about. It was so much fun hearing from her daughter and watching Laura open some of the things I had helped to handpick.

There's something special in knowing that someone cared enough to think not of your immediate needs, but your future needs. Sure, the toiletries, undergarments, and small stack of clothes are all necessities, and that's what most people thought of, when they thought of helping, but what most people didn't think about was, in a few weeks, when the dust had settled and the immediate helpers were gone or returned to their own lives, what would we need? To know that someone had thought of this and that that someone was me made me feel purposeful and worthy to still be alive.

Our town community center and multiple churches had set up donation centers around town. Each time I went, it was difficult to think of my own needs. Instead, when I saw boxes of children's shoes, because I had memorized the sizes for kids on our street, I would grab a box or a bucket of assorted cleaning supplies, or I'd add their names to the list of people needing help and reach-outs, because I knew they weren't able to add themselves.

Volunteer groups with heavy machinery were willing to clear out lots, including fallen trees, old footers and foundation remnants, and torn-up driveways ruined by the lifesaving equipment that had driven over and crushed them. Although it was amazing to have these opportunities, it was even more amazing to be able to put down the names and phone numbers of our neighbors who were dealing with hospitalized children and their own medical recoveries. I almost felt like a Neighborhood Watch person, but I watched for opportunities and made sure we shared them all.

* * *

In the backyard of our previous home, we had saved and saved and finally had enough to afford the small fortune it cost to fence in a quarter acre and allow our two crazy German Shepherds the freedom to chase balls wherever they pleased. It was wonderful, because we could spend time outdoors without worrying about the random squirrel or bird that would try to lure our babies away from our yard.

We'd found a wonderful local man, Mike, and his team to complete the fence, and it was truly beautiful work. We'd found solar lights on clearance, and Kory spent hours attaching them to every other fence post, to light up the backyard and give a fairy-like feel to our space. Of course, the fence was long gone after the storm. I couldn't imagine the force of the winds necessary to pull the cemented fence posts out of the ground and carry them away to some unknown place.

After the storm, the gentleman who completed our fence reached back out to us and asked to meet with us, along with some of our neighbors, because their church wanted to talk about ways that they could help us. We all were usually in the same area, so one Friday, we all got together. Dear Mike handed each family I had helped gather an envelope. Inside each was a sum of money that was beyond what we could have asked for, to allow us to help recover and to cover some immediate expenses that would take a while for insurance companies to get to.

I think the best feeling that day was giving away our own envelope to another family, because we had miscounted and invited too many people. We had been helped by so many, and passing that along felt like what God wanted me to do. God bless Mike's amazing fence and his caring church family who had thought of us.

* * *

Another way I focused my efforts after the storm was with my time. Multiple semi-truck loads full of donations had made their way to our local police department. The way we figured this out was when driving by one day, to check out why there were two big tents set up out front.

I spoke to a wonderful officer, who was running the entire operation. He was disappointed, because they had all of these donations and nobody was stopping by to take advantage of the help. Of course, things had begun closing around town about the same time and many families were displaced, so, given the lost jobs and lost wages, we knew there were plenty of people all around us who could benefit from the donations. The problem was, how do we reach them? It was especially touching to me, because an entire truckload was full of diapers, wipes, formula, and other baby items, things I wished I had needed.

While we were there, we grabbed a case of water and some snacks. Later that evening, I brainstormed to figure out what I could do. After a somewhat good night's sleep, I knew how I could help the officers distribute the donations. Word in a small town travels fast. I had social media friend requests from all over. I usually am pretty particular about whom I let into my life, but on this occasion, I accepted all of the requests. After that, I began posting.

I shared pictures and information about the donations wherever I could think to. Shortly after, people began to reach out.

"I could really use some diapers, but I can't leave my house."

There were so many people who could benefit from these things, so, as they began reaching out to me, I began to make a list. I noted the person, their address, what they needed, and how many people lived there. Then, I showed up to the big set of tents and semis. Me and two or three officers would get to work, compiling garbage bags full of goods. I would create a label with the address, attach it to a bag, and then the bags were loaded up into police cars and delivered throughout the county.

We unloaded almost an entire semi of baby gear that, otherwise, would have just sat there. Sometimes, Kory and I delivered the bags to the homes I knew were close to our temporary home. That was a really special thing, to be the deliverer of goods to those in need. I now knew what it was like to have needs.

Two important lessons I learned after the storm were that it's important to share the blessings God shares with you and no matter how hard you try, you can't outgive God.

CHAPTER 22

Good Intentions

1 Timothy 1:5: "The goal is love, which comes from a pure heart and a good conscience and a sincere faith."

Despite our perceptions, most people have good intentions. It may not always appear that way, but it's important that we don't judge based on our limited understandings.

Kory's return to work left me at home alone with the dogs, three to four days a week, waiting for him to finish his twelve-hour shifts. I spent my time working on house plans, going through recovered belongings, helping the police department distribute donations, and just getting our life back together in general. If I didn't drop him off at work at 6:45 a.m., I stayed at home without a vehicle to get around. But that was okay—I had loads to do. People thought that, because we had nothing, we wanted all the things that they didn't want.

People from all over town messaged me on Facebook Messenger, telling me they had things they wanted to donate to me and my neighbors. We had slowly started to accumulate things again, ourselves, but I readily agreed to be the main point of contact, because I had free time during the day. The stuff came to my front door filling garbage bags and boxes. I woke up each day to a new container to go through.

One would have expected us to have received things like clothes in our size, kitchen items anyone would need to begin a life again, and pragmatic things that just made sense. Unfortunately, that was not the case. Looking back, I know that people's hearts were in the right place, but sometimes, I wondered what the heck they were thinking.

I received an unfathomable amount of partial crystal glass sets, missing the final piece, so us leaving sets of 3 or 5 glasses. I got mismatched dish sets of all sorts and seasons. There were crystal serving plates mixed in with Christmas- and apple-themed partial dish sets. There were occasional bakeware pans, but most were dented, scratched, and bent—not something I wanted to start fresh with. Honestly, if I'd wanted partial sets of things or bent pieces, I would have dug them up from the ground at the lot where we used to live.

I began to sort, document, and post pictures of various donated items. Some of them were claimed by my neighbors and friends, so I would repackage them up, set them outside the front door, and alert the recipients that their things were ready. Some people were survivors who needed replacements, and some were just collectors of odd things.

Not only did I receive a plethora of kitchen items, I received at least fifteen black garbage bags full of clothes. You know those clothes that sit at the back of the closet, either in boxes or at the back of drawers, sometimes untouched for decades? Well, when a tornado happens and someone loses everything, some people think they should just get rid of all the things they don't want, so they drop them off for someone else to deal with.

Now, I'm sure this is not what went through many people's minds as they brought these things to my front door, but my friends and I had to laugh as we sorted through all the clothes. We found shirts from early-2000s Victoria's Secret collections and bedazzled jeans with rips and stains on them. I even received a Spandex set in bright, bold colors that I could only describe as traditional African garb; it currently sits in the back of my own closet, because it was so unique, I couldn't get rid of it.

I received many stained, ripped, used, and unloved clothes, too. Over time, the donations and process of sorting them started to wear on me. Did other people consider me only worthy of their own discarded and unwanted items? If they didn't want these things, what made them think *I* did? I learned two really important lessons that day, and thankfully, God was able to change my heart.

One, most people have good intentions. They wanted to help, so they got that box of clothes or kitchen dishes they no longer used and brought them promptly to me, probably thinking, well, having something is better than nothing! Their intentions were mostly good. I had to remind myself that the value of these things did not represent the value people thought about me.

The second thing I learned is, if anyone ever needed anything and I was able to provide, I would give them some of my favorite items out of my own closet, or I would buy them something new. I would want them to feel valued and cherished, like they were worth having some of my best things. That or I would just get them a gift card and let them pick out what they wanted in the correct size.

* * *

I love to cook. I'm pretty sure I got that trait from my momma, because she started teaching me how to scramble eggs when I was two years old. Baking Christmas cookies was always a huge deal. We didn't just make your typical sugar cookies and dump all the sprinkles on top. We made peppermint candy-cane twists, Russian tea cakes, magic cookie bars, and my personal favorite, M&M

meringues. It got to the point where I stopped asking which ingredients went next... I just knew.

Well, thank goodness I learned those kitchen skills, because my husband always tells me it was one of the top-five reasons he married me! I remember how, in grad school on those late study nights, we would chop up some chicken and vegetables and make some quinoa or rice, preparing our meals together before we sat down for our endless study sessions. The longer we were married, the more recipes I learned, more cookbooks I acquired, and more Pinterest boards I made.

We had our favorites, like avocado and goat-cheese-stuffed meatloaf, lemon piccata chicken, and champagne risotto. We had friends over for dinner and created an assembly line of people who loaded up their plates before sitting on the floor in the living room or on the couch and enjoying everyone's company while we ate as a big, extended family.

Well, after the tornado, cooking became more of a chore than an enjoyment. Not only did I no longer have my cookbooks and pots and pans, but I didn't have those nuanced ingredients hanging out in my pantry, like capers, chili sauce, and vanilla extract. The beautiful cottage we were staying at had your basic salt, pepper, and two to three more kitchen spices, but every time I went to make a dish we loved, I became more and more discouraged, hunting and wishing for my ingredients to show back up. After a while, I just stopped trying.

God knew this would happen. That's when we started receiving gift cards in the mail. Our mail had been delayed for a while, because, obviously, we didn't have a mailbox anymore. We had family members send things to a close friend of ours, and she was such a blessing, collecting my birth certificate, sent from my mother, holding packages sent by friends, and allowing us to use her home as our address to order from Amazon and other stores.

Well, we finally got around to the post office. We had received letters from numerous friends who shared their condolences but who also enclosed meal tickets in the form of gift cards to local restaurants. God always knows what you need before you even know to ask for it.

Those were almost as good as the emails we received with Door Dash and delivery service e-certificates. This break from cooking allowed us to stay fed while using little brain power and helped us to inventory what we would really start to need.

At some point, we had to create our own Amazon list. My mom told me it was great how I was trying so hard to help others get their lives restarted, but our friends really wanted to help *me* out, too. So, late one night, Kory and I split a bottle of wine and started a list.

Man, that was a hard thing to do. What do you order or request first? Do you buy kitchen things? Do you ask for clothes? What about bath towels, picture frames, and trash cans? We didn't yet have a place to live—we were still in the cabin before moving into the short-term rental, and Megan's house could only hold so many boxes.

I remember being very intentional about the things we added to our wishlist, making sure not to add pots and pans or bath towels until I could get to a store to feel how soft they were or could read reviews online, and at that time, those tasks seemed too daunting. We skipped those and opted for a couple of coffee mugs, a basket to organize our belongings and make them easier to move, a laundry hamper, Crocs, and a rug to go in front of our temporary bed, so the dogs could jump up more easily. I got some headbands, cookbooks, wine glasses, and a coffee pot. You know, necessities.

But those things were bought for us quickly.

It wasn't until we got into our rental a month later that I really felt comfortable beginning our rebuilding. Then came the Pyrex, the pantry organizational sets, and baking sheets. I finally allowed myself to order the things I knew I would need to replace my previous kitchen and allow me to start cooking again.

During this time of picking the things I wanted, I received four or five packages of things I didn't specifically ask for, without a name attached to them. They were some big-ticket items, including white bath towels, a pot-and-pan kitchen set, and a set of dishes that were simple, white, and beautiful.

I know it's odd and ungrateful, but I immediately got angry when I received these gifts. These were *not* things I had asked for and *not* the specific brands and sizes I wanted. Part of me appreciated the thought, but mostly, I was just mad.

Looking back, I am so grateful to whoever sent me all of those secret gifts, because, first of all, they truly knew me. They knew I'd want white, basic towels, white and simple dishes, and stainless steel pots and pans. They knew I hadn't put these things on my Amazon list, but that I would need them, and they were right.

Over time, I grew to greatly appreciate the gifts, and I regretted the anger that had initially filled my heart. I hope whoever that was knows how much those things meant to me.

CHAPTER 23

What's a Pandemic?

Colossians 3:23: "Whatever you do, work at it with all your heart, as working for the Lord, not for human masters."

A big reason Kory went back to work so soon was because his job as a nurse was highly needed. People were sick everywhere. He went back because it was the right thing to do, by God's word. Both of us worked in the medical field, exposing ourselves to sickness, because it's what we were called to do.

As time passed, we focused on what was in front of us, which included finishing our rebuild, refurnishing our lives, and stocking up on items we would need once we moved out of our convenient rental. Something else that came with time was returning to work, but that's not as simple as it sounds.

The day of the storm, Kory and I both expected to be at work in the morning, and with the spotty cell phone service, we both had limited ability to connect with our companies. I was able to get a text through to my boss at 4 a.m., although I have no recollection of actually sending it.

I didn't beat around the bush and was very blunt: *Our house is gone, and so is most of our neighborhood. I won't be in today. Kory and I are alive, my phone isn't taking calls.*

When I sent the text, I had no idea that the whole town didn't know what had happened the night before. And why would they? We didn't have a local news team to cover it, and Nashville news was over an hour away. Because of this, though, I didn't mention our losing our house or the fact that a tornado had just ripped through my front door and taken it along for a ride.

My boss was instantly sympathetic toward our situation and asked what she could do, as did so many other. Really, I had no idea. All I could do was send a picture of the house that no longer stood, now reduced to piles of rubble. I also had to explain that I didn't have a car to facilitate me working. I worked in home health and at one point had covered up to seven surrounding counties in a week's time, which was totally not doable without a car. I also no longer had my tablet, which was my way to document all my medical notes and carried earlier notes and consent forms I had taken at previous visits. Even if the stars had aligned and all of those things were available to me, I was in no condition to drive, much less work.

When I texted my boss at 4 a.m., only two hours after the storm, Kory was not with me, because he was out helping to save and assist as many people as he could. He also did not have a phone, as it was lost somewhere in the rubble of our destroyed home. By the time we made it to lunch with our family later that day, we finally remembered to call his work to let them know he wouldn't be in to work that day, obviously. And also, to let them know we were both alive.

He called from a family member's phone. When they answered and he said, "This is Kory," the nurse on the other end of the line almost dropped the phone. They had seen our neighbors admitted to the hospital and to their very floor for post-surgical recovery, but nobody had heard from us until that moment. I can only imagine the relief that came over her, as she shared with her coworkers that we were alive and mostly uninjured.

We both applied for FMLA, due to the traumatic event and our need to recover and get our lives together before returning. Once we had gotten into some sort of routine again and were settled into our rental house, we decided that Kory would return to work only six short weeks after the storm.

We made this decision for a few reasons. One, we needed to make money again. Our expenses were low and our rent was paid for by insurance, but we still had daily needs for food, gas, and other bills. I still didn't have a vehicle, so I couldn't yet go back, and although I was feeling more comfortable, I didn't want to spend my days behind the wheel, navigating the countryside, as my home health job required. Kory also worked as a nurse at the hospital and on the floor that became our town's covid unit, and they were slammed. Kory is, by trade, a caregiver, and his heart is in helping others, so he felt drawn to return and relieve his coworkers of their great burden. Finally, we needed to get back to some sense of normalcy, and this seemed like the next step.

We faced some obstacles before this was even a possibility. We would need scrubs, a stethoscope for Kory, and appropriate shoes. I don't really recall where these items came from, but I think his mom helped us source them. It all became truly real, though, when he went into the human resources department to get a new badge. When he came home, I think I finally realized I'd been left alone for twelve-plus hours at a time, when he went back to work.

* * *

The tornado hit our quiet little street on March 3, 2020. Most people remember that year and this time period as the start to what we hoped would be a short period of quarantine, but which really turned into years of fear and a lifetime of resulting changes to our society. It's funny, because, looking back at that time, the first thing to come to my mind is not things like quarantining, wearing masks, or worrying about toilet paper. For me, it is my many memories of frustration.

I was frustrated that I couldn't order the things I needed offline. When covid hit, only "essentials" were being prioritized and sent to people across the country. Well, first of all, can someone please tell me what the heck is considered essential, when you literally have *nothing*? I remember trying to get clothes or kitchen items and being told the wait time would be weeks to months. What may, under different circumstances, seem like a reasonable time period felt completely unrealistic to me and made me so angry, because didn't they know I was just trying to put my life back together?

I was also frustrated because I couldn't relate to other people. While my friends and family across the nation had worries about public health and protecting their families, my focus was solely on living in the moment and surviving. I had the hardest time understanding why I couldn't see my friends and family when, after losing almost everything else in my life, the community and social interaction were what Kory and I needed the most.

In the early stages of the pandemic, not a whole lot was known about how the virus spread. Could we be outside together? Could we be inside with masks on? What if I stayed six feet apart, was that really enough? What was the truth and what was exaggerated by people who didn't know what they were talking about? Who really knew what they were talking about, anyway?

Living in a small, partially rural town in the middle of Tennessee meant we had a lot of people who went about their daily lives, regardless of what was going on. Rules were constantly changing at the hospital where Kory returned to work, too. At first, you couldn't wear a mask because it might scare the patients. Then, you had to wear a mask, but there was a shortage, so they were required to keep them in a brown paper bag that would surely fester, allowing any residual bacteria to which it was exposed to grow in the moist environment. Then it was full gowns and N95 masks, and most of the time, they didn't have the right size either.

You see, if you don't work in the medical field, you wouldn't know that, in order for a true N95 mask to work, it has to be fitted so securely to your face that they test you to make sure of it. The test involves donning the already tight mask, placing a hood over your shoulders, and then the tester sprays a sweet-smelling solution into the hood. If you can taste or smell even the slightest hint of sweetness, the mask has failed, and you must try another size. This is a mandatory part of hiring for any medical company or hospital where I have ever worked, yet, when there is a shortage, you're supposed to take what you can get and use it the best you can. All in all, the masks weren't doing their job, and the nurses and medical staff knew it. But once again, what could you do?

It's the same as when you get a patient with tuberculosis. You put on the equipment required, go into the negative-pressure hospital room, and hope to God you don't catch something or take it home to your family. The pandemic was nothing new to the nurses as far as diseases went. No, where we saw the most impact, at least from what I could tell from the stories from Kory and his coworkers, was from the lack of support. This included the lack of support regarding equipment and understaffing, as well as the lack of support for patients and their families.

When Kory went back to work, he was thrown into the daily bump and grind of a grueling twelve-hour shift, but he was also thrown into the unknown of dealing with the virus and the death and destruction that followed it. Every day, he was faced with new policies rolled out by the hospital, as it tried to keep its employees safe. He was faced with people who could barely breathe, despite countless interventions. He was faced with holding the hands of people who had to die alone, without their families; some maybe had a rough Facetime call, but even then, the families couldn't hear or communicate over the noise of the breathing machines attached to their loved ones.

It wasn't enough for Kory to experience the trauma and aftermath of the tornado. Then, he was thrown into the slow trauma of helping the sick as they passed on into the next life. There was no reprieve for him, and I have no idea how he faced it. Every. Single. Day.

It's not a surprise, then, that when he came home, we didn't talk about what he had dealt with every day. Who wants to relive those memories? Instead, we carried on with our life as best we could, dealing with the trauma that surrounded us in any ways we could.

* * *

Eventually, I had to return to work, too. I had taken the full three months allotted for my FMLA leave, and I had finally gotten a vehicle. Financially, I still had crippling student debt to pay off, so back to work it was.

The fear of returning was so great for me. I knew from the little Kory had told me that people were being sent home from the hospital in situations we normally would never allow. However, with so many sick and not enough space at the hospitals, what could be done? The nursing homes were overflowing, and many of them weren't taking covid patients, in an attempt to keep their current residents as safe as possible. Because of all of these extenuating circumstances, people were being sent home and into my realm.

As a home health physical therapist, it was my job to attempt to rehab these people back to their highest potential. I was very familiar with debilitated people, since I had been dealing with it for five years at that point. What I wasn't familiar with was dealing with, and still healing from my own trauma, while facing another huge change. I was expected to go into people's houses, many times as the first clinician, to go over medications, assess the safety of their home, and then provide physical therapy assessment and interventions, and do it all while covered head-to-toe in supposedly protective wear that I had to put on and take off at each home. This included an ugly, yellow, disposable gown, shoe covers, a head cover, gloves, an N95 mask, goggles, and a face shield. This was all on top of my own scrubs.

Sure, safety first, I get it. But what you don't understand is how some people live. You see, I went into the boonies and backwoods of Tennessee. Sometimes, I would drive over an hour just to get to one home. There would be no cell phone service, no backup, and no help if I blew a tire. No bathrooms, no gas stations, no nothing. Sometimes, I'd pull up to an old, dilapidated farmhouse without air conditioning and no indoor plumbing.

I've been to the homes of people in their eighties without living children or parents, who maybe lived with a sibling who was also older and had difficulty caring for them. Sometimes, there were holes in the floor, doors that didn't shut, and sometimes, the homes didn't even have doors on the frames, leaving the outdoors coming in. I never knew the hand I'd been dealt until I arrived: when you're the evaluating therapist, nobody goes before you to warn you.

The hardest part, though, was how often people didn't have air conditioning. In the heat of the summer, without AC, wearing all this clothing, it got hot fast. Sometimes, I had to spend up to two hours in a home, admitting someone into homecare and figuring out how I could safely leave them, counting on them to take their medication correctly without messing up so they didn't end up back in the hospital for an overdose or underdose.

I had to educate people not to smoke while wearing their oxygen. I kid you not, I had a patient who blew himself up, not once but two separate times, and then he still continued to smoke! Don't worry, we refused to go inside, if oxygen was on and the cigarette was lit, but we still had to knock on the door and check on him.

Working in home health had always been hard, but going back under these stressful conditions, with people in the worst shape I'd ever seen, that was extra hard. There was zero chance we could allow ourselves to let this pandemic take us over at home and in our private lives, too. Many times, it was easier to just pretend it didn't exist.

When people ask me about those years of recovery, I hardly ever consider that there was a pandemic happening, too, except that it was super-inconvenient. It was all we could do to shield ourselves from any more trauma than we'd already had to deal with.

CHAPTER 24

Growing Faith

Proverbs 3:5-6: "Trust in the Lord with all your heart and lean not on your own understanding; in all your ways, submit to Him, and He will make your paths straight."

Faith is not a straight line uphill. It is full of twists and turns, doubt and fear, gains and losses. Our faith is challenged daily by the one who doesn't want us to have a relationship with God. We always want "proof" of holiness, but in reality, faith is supposed to be based on what we cannot see but we feel. We must trust that God knows more than we do and will lead us in the right way.

I'm not a big movie or TV person; to be honest, I haven't been to a movie theater in close to five years. It took me an entire decade to watch *Frozen.* I just sit and laugh with my friends or husband when they quote movies or talk about what's playing now. I can quote *Anchor Man* with the best of them, and I remember *Finding Nemo* scenes for some odd reason, but I usually tap out when friends want to watch a movie, or I find something else to do when my husband asks if I want to watch something at home with him.

That being said, when I find something that I do like, I'm all in. My favorite movie of all time is *A Walk to Remember* based on the novel by Nicholas Sparks. The innocence of Mandy Moore's character, the cuteness of Shane West, and the ridiculously sappy love story all get to me in a way I can't describe. I will literally watch that movie over almost any other.

One of my favorite quotes from that movie is in the middle, when Shane has started to fall in love with Mandy, and he asks her about her devout faith. After some thought, she tells him, "It's like the wind—I can't see it, but I can feel it." Ever since hearing this quote, I can think of no better way to describe faith.

I haven't always felt this way about faith, God, and believing in a higher power. I wasn't raised in a church, and the closest thing to religion we got was spending weekends on the island, fishing off the bow of the boat, and wondering where all the beauty had come from. Easter was a day of chocolate, Christmas was a day of presents and the cinnamon rolls my mom would bake from scratch, and "Jesus music" was rather annoying, when my friend's mother played it in the car after picking us up from school and taking us to gymnastics practice.

At one point, I did become a Christian, but I had no idea what that meant. My mom had started taking us to a church with some other gymnastics families, and I went through a year's worth of confirmation classes with other preteens, but I don't remember a single thing they taught us there. The first big Christian influence I remember having in my life was when I got dropped off at school early so my mom could get to work, and I decided to go to a morning meeting in a portable classroom. They sang songs and then a guy would have us bow our heads and ask us to raise our hand if we didn't know God but wanted to. I remember them praying a prayer over me each and every week, after I raised my hand. Each and every week, I raised it again and again, because each time, I felt no different.

I didn't know how I was supposed to feel. I didn't feel lighter, happier, or more knowledgeable about God. I knew the songs a little better each time, but that was about it. I didn't know anything about the Bible, except that they were found in the pews at church, and I really didn't understand much about what was read aloud. My gymnastics friends went to church, so I asked my mom to take me, too, because it was what the other girls did.

We started going to church occasionally, when we weren't out of town traveling for gymnastics or at the beach and on the island. It became a place I started to like, but I had trouble fitting in at. At one point, our church decided to start a program where an anonymous person would send us encouraging letters and gifts. I don't remember why they did this, and I never found out who sent me mine, but she changed my life.

She sent me stickers, notes, letters, books, and arts and crafts. Soon, the tub under my bed was filled with potpourri and sweet-smelling things, plus all the letters she ever wrote to me. I felt seen, and I knew I wanted more of this. I don't remember if it was coincidence or if I asked, but we started going to church more often. That sweet, sweet woman made me feel loved by someone who had no reason to love me. That was my first true Christian experience of love and faith.

As time passed, I started going to youth group meetings, and I became more a part of weekly Bible studies. I grew to love our youth minister and felt she really saw me for the shy kid I was. She understood when we had to miss weekends for traveling competitions, and she supported my successes through gymnastics.

I was invited to church camps and youth group events, and I found a new group of amazing friends outside of gymnastics. Our youth minister was such a kind and loving soul, when the day came that I found out she was leaving, I was devastated. But gymnastics kept happening, life went on, and we missed a few more weekends at church.

My first weekend back with the new leader was eventful and life-changing. I remember I was getting ready to enter the door for youth group when this stocky, short-haired woman said, "Hi. You must be Lauren. Nice of you to finally show up."

Wait, *what?* Where was the kindness and love? Where was the gratefulness to see me and welcome me? Where was the sense of belonging?

It all fell away, just like my confidence, and my heart dropped. I immediately wanted to hide behind someone or skulk away, embarrassed. But embarrassed for what? What was this negative quality this woman saw in me after just meeting me?

Oh, she saw me. She saw when I wasn't there, and she called me out for it, in front of all of my new friends. I felt instant embarrassment. Later that night, I asked my mom never to take me back.

Looking back, I know she was probably being sarcastic and just trying to joke around, to get me to open up, but I felt raw, misunderstood, and unsupported in my gymnastics career. I knew I never wanted to feel like that again.

I know there are so many of us who go through similar circumstances when it comes to the church. Whether we are called out, feel unsupported, or are misunderstood in our church families, we feel pushed away and unloved. Something that took me years and years to understand was that, usually, this is unintentional. Most Christians do not go out of their way to hurt us, and if they do, it's not about some problem they have with *us.*

You see, as Christians, we are perceived by the outside world as feeling justified to judge and point fingers whenever others commit wrongs. In fact, Christians are just as fallible as any other human and have no leg up or special "in" with God when it comes to our mistakes and forgiveness. Our pride, arrogance, and envy frequently get in the way of our desire to demonstrate God's love to the outside world and, sometimes, even to our church family. We can misunderstand, speak out of line, and mess up just like the rest of humanity. It's easy to push people away but oh so difficult to pull them back in with love. This is something I experienced firsthand.

After that, I found different avenues for involvement, including joining the right Christian groups in high school and calling myself a Christian in college, when, in reality, I was not practicing Christian faith, demonstrating God's love, or pursuing a godly life. I learned to shotgun a beer, show off my figure in certain clothes, and pass my classes well enough in college. I prayed occasionally, like when I needed a stomach ache to go away or wanted to score enough on a test to keep my scholarship, even to have my crush call me, but that wasn't real prayer and faith.

I actually didn't get back to my religion and faith until my future husband entered my life. Kory was raised the opposite of me. He went to church twice a week, went to a Christian private school for twelve years, and spent his first year of college at a Christian one. But something we had in common was our ability to outwardly seem like we were good Christian people. Things like joining the right clubs, saying an occasional prayer, and going to church when he went home. These were all boxes he checked off.

Things didn't change for him when he went to graduate school. Like a good Christian boy, he reported to his mom that he was looking for a church home while he was away at school. And he stayed true to his word, because, despite his come-and-go relationship with the Lord, he definitely was not a liar, especially not to his momma. Well, as his girlfriend, I was not going to give up valuable weekend time, so off to church we went.

We sang the songs, said the prayers, and, without my knowing, God began to work in my heart. You see, the more you surround yourself and immerse yourself in an environment, the more it envelops you. This is true with bad situations, too. If you hang out with people who party and do drugs and listen to degrading and slurring music, you begin to embrace it as part of your identity. I'm lucky I was pulled in the direction of Kory, because God came back into my heart.

Now, we weren't perfect. We still drank too much sometimes and fought way too loudly with each other over silly things, both of us unable to put our pride and arrogance aside, but the beautiful thing about God is His timing. The love in my heart and the desire for Him continued to spread each Sunday.

I'm so fortunate for that, because the time came when things didn't work out for Kory and he left grad school without finishing. While leaving behind school and physical therapy, he was determined to leave behind any memory of the place, including me. We had been together for a year at that point and were in love. When he told me we were done, I couldn't believe he would throw it all away just because of an eight-hour drive and reliance on phone calls for communication.

Now, I knew he had a lot of self-discovery to do and would be busy paying back his dad and applying to nursing schools to pursue the next phase of his life, but I also knew I couldn't be without him. In an effort to save my heart from any more breaking, I offered the only thing I knew he couldn't turn down. I offered to not bother him during the day, but just spend five minutes a night reading the Bible with him.

My intentions were not pure. I didn't not have the desire to learn more about God and fill my soul with Jesus, which I clearly needed, but I knew that Kory's good-heartedness and momma's-boy attitude wouldn't turn me down, and he didn't. For weeks, we didn't talk or text during the day. Then, before bed, we stayed up for just five minutes, reading together. I had never read the Bible outside of church or Bible study, except for maybe a passage here or there, so I had no idea what I was getting myself into.

We started from the beginning and just started to read. Genesis was first, then Exodus followed by books I'd never heard of before. Some of it got really boring, and we tended to skip over chapters of names, ages, and long listings of people. Then, a little at a time, our conversations grew longer.

Since I had never read this before, I had a ton of questions. Since he had been brought up in Christian schools his whole life, he had a ton of answers, even if some of them took time for him to remember or to relearn answers from other sources. We grew more and more together and learned the way it was before God sent His son. We learned about sacrifice and the old ways and things I'd never been exposed to before. Slowly, day by day, Kory opened up to dating me again.

We started texting and visiting, and I felt like I had my boyfriend back again, but a way better version. I kept going to church without him, and although, in the beginning, I tried to use God's word to manipulate Kory into staying in contact with me, God used His word to encourage my closeness to Him. He also used it to rebuild our relationship on the basis of faith, without the physical contact we were so used to having. I began to grow my faith and see beauty as a gift from God. This is especially easy to do when you live a block from the ocean and can witness the beautiful sunrises and sunsets on a regular basis. God's beauty was all around me, but I had never had my eyes opened wide enough to see.

When we got married and I moved to a new state to be with my new husband, we continued our practice of religion and set off to find a church home for us. We found one that Kory had belonged to during his previous time at the University, doing his undergrad degree before he met me, but it was the best fit for us.

We went to church on Sundays and tried to come back Sunday evenings for singing services and ice cream socials, but it was really very hard for me to feel like I belonged. I still felt like I was treated like a college student, and this infuriated me, because didn't they know I was twenty-six and had a doctorate? I was not a college student, I didn't live like a college student, and I did not want to be treated as a college student.

Somebody saw my angst, or perhaps I was the catalyst for a long-standing problem, so a Sunday morning class was created for us to participate in and co-lead, made up of just a few other misfit people. It included a young family, a couple who were four years younger than we were, which, to be honest, felt like a lifetime younger, and a single guy who was a little older than us. There were some others who came and went, as well. We had great discussions but didn't hang out much outside of that group on Sunday mornings.

I continued to feel like a misfit's group, without identity and without a feeling of belonging, so my fire and fury toward the church to fit in and have a place to settle grew. As someone who wears every emotion on her face, it became hard to conceal my disdain for lack of placement. I targeted my anger toward the leaders and could hardly look them in the eye when they passed by.

I remember how once, during some reorganization, they were moving around classrooms and took our group's classroom away.

Our spot had been located in the kids' hallway, which was already a hard pill for me to swallow, and it was used for a photography classroom for a couple of months. We were then displaced to a library meeting room.

Although it had an awesome official vibe to it and I got to lose my thoughts in reading older, outdated book titles, it still didn't feel like a room for us. It felt like a dusty, makeshift place, with our small group stretched around a large meeting table. Then, we were moved again, but this time to the college area, full circle in my opinion. This just continued to make me feel more and more disposable, as we were jostled around from place to place. Not only did I not fit in with the congregation, who always milled around before church each Sunday, greeting one another and saying hello, but the group they created for us wasn't even allowed to fit in.

Have you ever felt so mad at a church member or leader or at a congregation in general that you thought you were going to burst into flames and go to hell yourself? Yeah, that's the anger I found building inside of me. Looking back, I realize they probably didn't even know this anger existed. How many times do we let something fester, burn, and grow inside of us without ever addressing the problem?

Well, despite my feelings and despite my resentment, God knew what He was doing. During this period of my anger and feeling like a misfit, He began to show me what belonging really looked like. I learned a big lesson during this, not all at once, but over time. I realized, if you never give yourself the opportunity to become a part of a group, if you're constantly segregating yourself and then getting mad at others for not doing a good job of involving you, then you're doing it wrong.

Involvement and inclusion aren't gifts that people receive by chance. They come from effort, through putting yourself out there and trying new things around new people. You have to be willing to get involved and be exposed to newness, resolution, and integration before you will ever feel like you belong somewhere.

Looking back, I never made an effort to explore the "adult" Sunday school classes. I saw other young married couples around the church, but where did they go on Sunday mornings before service? If I had just taken the time to enquire about different groups, or to walk around and try out different classes each morning, I would have met a lot of great people a lot faster. I would have taken initiative to solve the angst and off-puttedness I was feeling. Why did I rely so heavily on other people to find my place to fit in?

Sometime after we joined our church, the women in leadership embarked on starting an amazing program called "Heartfelt Sisters," which is a nationwide movement to bring the older women of the church together with the younger women. The grandmother-like figures took on mothers who were in the middle of raising their families, along with other young women, and they served and loved them. It really is a wonderful idea. Groups were assigned for a year. Once a month, the younger women attended a dinner at the older women's homes, where they were served and taken care of.

Well, I didn't know many of the people who were signing up, but I decided to take a leap and join a group. Not only did I join a group, I had to do it alone, without Kory! I'm so glad I did, because this movement led to such a beautiful relationship, one I never would have been able to experience without this program.

Finally, I started feeling seen. Finally, someone wanted to hear my opinion and help me grow my faith. I had a group of women whom I would eventually grow to respect, who listened to my hard questions and tried their best to help me find answers, or at least to find peace in my heart. The simple act of not being allowed to do so much as pour my own drink gave me an outlet and an opportunity to feel appreciated and to begin working on my inner peace around my disgruntlement.

My frustrations did not grow in this environment, although they did continue to exist. I was not always fully satisfied with the answers, which I often felt were "meek and mild," but little did I even realize these were some of the strongest women I'd ever meet, because of their ability to remain humble, prideless, and content. I gained a new perspective on understanding and was able to appreciate the beauty of traditions I was not raised with, but that existed, regardless.

This beautiful relationship didn't just end with each meal. It continued on into each Sunday morning gathering before our morning service. Now, I had people to look for before church started on Sundays. I had people who were excited to see me, women who sought me out or caught my eye in a crowd and gave me a truly meaningful hug, once they reached me. They cared about me, listened to my stories of infertility and discontent with women's position in the church, and prayed for all the big and small things alike. This began my big shift, transitioning from the fringe of religion to true acclimation and involvement in what it means to be practicing a religion. I was being seen, but not just seen, I was being heard.

The next way we began to further integrate into becoming a part of our church family was by getting involved with a small group in our neighborhood. That was an ultimate game-changer. We grew close to our neighbors, and they helped me sort through my struggles, helping me to feel like an adult and actual member of the church. More new perspectives from men and women were shared, and we became family. We had bimonthly dinners and Bible studies, we carved pumpkins and threw holiday parties, and we called one another to borrow a cup of sugar or help dig a hole for a new tree. We continued to belong, and with this new sense of belonging came a root system that began to take hold.

Despite our growth in our local church community and joining a small group, Kory and I began to visit friends in South Carolina, look at property in Florida near my parents, and even explore other parts of Tennessee, near his parents. We didn't have roots where we lived, and since Kory had graduated college for the second time, we could go anywhere. Nurses and physical therapists were always needed everywhere. With each new property search or night spent looking at house plans, we began to feel more detached from our church family, our community, and the roots we had allowed to take hold.

Then, the storm hit, and everything changed: our resources, our desires, our hearts, and our relationship with God. All of it changed for the better, which is really crazy to say, because we didn't have a bad life before at all, but what we really lacked was direction.

When you lose it all and have so much opportunity to leave, it takes a strong pull to keep you rooted where you are, especially when the roots aren't strong to begin with. The crazy thing is it's not the strength of our roots that mattered, it was the richness of the soil and our community around us. It was God's way of showing us that we were exactly where we needed to be, even if that meant we stayed in a town farther away from our families.

After the storm, we could have gone anywhere. We didn't have a house to sell, and we had the cash from our investment into the property and the work we had done on the home. We could afford the property in the Carolinas or Florida. We could do anything. So, Why. Did. We. Stay? The question was simple, and the answer was simple, but the reasoning is what makes our story so unique.

Okay, back to the *why*. Well, the short answer is our faith. We felt drawn to our community, to healing with our neighbors, and to understanding why this had happened to us. I'd stopped believing in coincidences a long time ago.

Why was our street, the street where three of the ministry leaders from our church lived, hit from this storm cell with the hardest force of any other area? Why were the babies on this street hit and affected the most? Why was the beautiful family of three just a few houses down all taken away on that night?

You see, when God's people get together, put their complete trust in Him, and practice loving their neighbors with all of their heart, they put a target on their backs. They let the evil know exactly where we are, because one light shines in the dark, but a handful of lights shine like a beacon, calling others toward it. Even calling those who don't have a good purpose and whose only aim is to destroy the light.

When we experienced our trauma from that night, we were not alone. God fought for us the entire time and never left our side. He provided me with two pairs of shoes to protect our feet. He provided Kory and me with the ability to remain calm and maintain synchronization without having to say a word to each other. We knew we had survived and been spared from injury to help others and we were able to help so many that night. We were given a story to share. A story of hope that allows others to see that, no matter the storm you are faced with, there is always God's presence to get you through it and hope for a better future, when you come out of it.

My friend asked me when did my faith really shift and when was I able to lean into my ability to trust in God's plan for me. It was after the night He gave me all the protection my feet needed.

CHAPTER 25

Tragedy Creates Bonds

1 Peter: 8-10: "Above all, love each other deeply, because love covers over a multitude of sins. Offer hospitality to one another without grumbling. Each of you should use whatever gift you have received to serve others, as faithful stewards of God's grace in its various forms."

No matter the past or what ill-will you may be keeping pent up, there is always a chance to mend friendships, if you can humble yourself and allow love to take over your heart. God brings us friends and help when we need it, but the only way that happens is when we open our hearts to them.

After the storm, we endured the pandemic and were faced with isolation, fear, and so many unknowns. We were isolated from people, friends, and community, and it was so difficult to endure another setback to recovery. However, through all of this, God blessed me with new friendships.

Let me start back to over ten years ago, to a time when I didn't even know my husband. In my eyes, he should have no past, no dating history, and never have kissed anyone but me, right? Well, even though that may not be the truth, it's hard to imagine anything but that, when you marry someone. You see, I don't like to label myself as the jealous type, but looking back, I was a hundred percent the epitome of the jealous type.

I remember back to our dating days at grad school in Florida, when we first claimed an official relationship title and began hanging out together with friends and classmates. If a girl got too close during a conversation or leaned in to tell Kory a joke, I became heated to my core and enraged that someone would dare to interact with my future husband! Because I knew early on that, of course, we would get married someday! I remember going to the beach with our group and noticing how one girl in particular got just a little too flirty with my Kory.

I used to be super-hotheaded, and I knew how some girls could be toward a claimed man. In my eyes, he was bait and the other girls were lionesses, stalking their targeted prey. Looking back, I get pretty embarrassed with myself at my own thoughts and behavior, but it definitely makes me appreciate how far I've come in that department.

Before I grew to be the more chilled-out version of myself that I am today, I dealt with those feelings of insecurity with a rage-filled hate for one of Kory's previous girlfriends, after Kory and I were married and had moved to Tennessee, away from prying eyes of those Florida girls. Enter this beautiful young woman, whom I'll call Kate. Kate and Kory had been on mission trips together in their younger years and ended up dating for a short period of time before they broke it off. Then, he went to Florida, where he met me.

Kate ended up moving to our town, and low and behold, she became a member of our church, which she had attended with Kory, before I'd met him. I remember the anger that boiled inside of me whenever I saw her smiling face.

Of course, since we were about the same age and went to the same church, we had a similar circle of friends, so we crossed paths frequently on Sunday mornings and sometimes even out in town. I don't think I ever even spoke a word to her, but I did my best to offer the smallest, most meager smile I could muster. The negative feelings I had for her were unexplainable, but I could not physically control the increase of my heart rate or my clenched jaw in her presence.

As you can see, I wasn't her biggest fan, but really, it was through no fault of her own. The craziest part of it all is that she was happily married and had a baby on the way! How could I hold so much hate and distaste for someone I had no history with and had no real reason to dislike?

One memory that was difficult for me was when one of Kory's best friends from college got married. Kory was, of course, asked to be in the wedding. The problem was, Kate was a close friend of theirs and was asked to be in the wedding party, too. I remember thinking to myself I would lose my ever-loving mind if Kory and Kate walked down that dang aisle together. Thankfully, they didn't, and I only had to endure her presence from afar on that day, which should have been just a joyful celebration.

Fast forward to three days after the storm., Kory and I were in the heat of recovering, finding shelter, getting essential items, and trying to keep our sanity. The wonderful people of our town were heavily involved in recovery efforts and were posting lost items that had landed in their yards all over social media, tagging Kory and me in them. I could not keep track of everything, and at the time, Kory didn't even have a phone, so I was doing double duty, trying to claim personal items I wanted back, but trying to manage getting a new driver's license and sourcing a rental car, along with other urgent tasks.

One day, as I was checking my messages, amongst the mass reach-outs from people offering help, one in particular stood out.

Kate. She had messaged me to tell me she would be in town, and asked if there was anything she could do for us or pick up for us.

The years of rage and anger I had built up in my heart for this woman all of a sudden vanished. Just like the tornado winds that had brought all of their fury onto us that night, my feelings disappeared just as quickly as the storm.

I have no explanation for it, except that my broken heart was so overwhelmed with everything going on, I just didn't have the space for hate anymore. God had completely cleared my heart, my memory of discomfort about her, and had instead filled it with gratefulness that yet another person was reaching out to lend a hand.

Ironically, the first thing I asked her to do was to help me look for my wedding dress, as one had been turned in at the Sheriff's department. Kory's ex-girlfriend, whom I had hated for so long, was going to look for one of the most sacred items a girl keeps after she becomes a wife. The irony didn't even phase me at the moment, but it is a memory I will think about for the rest of my life.

We continued to grow closer and work together in the weeks after the storm. Not only did Kate help me, but she helped me help others. One particular memory I have is when I heard about a Hispanic family that had been greatly affected by the storm. They had no insurance or means of recovery, and their situation was also hampered by their inability to speak English.

I don't even remember how I came across this knowledge about them, but I immediately called Kate. She was fluent in Spanish and agreed to come translate with me. We didn't even have the exact address and I didn't have a car, so she picked me up, and we drove the streets of a nearby neighborhood, looking for their damaged car that had been described to us.

When we found the house, we tentatively knocked on the door, and the man answered by just barely cracking it open. Kate was able to translate, and he let us into the foyer. She explained that we'd heard he needed help and we wanted to try to meet some of his needs.

Something we had learned was that their microwave no longer worked, so replacing it became my mission. I wanted to support a local business and supply this family with the best microwave I could. We went to the local DT McCall's furniture and appliance store and got them a nicer microwave than I have now. Kate drove me there, we dropped it off, and with it, I gave them enough cash to cover the damage to their car, so they could still get around and to work.

I don't remember the family, their reactions, or whether they were grateful or not, although I'm sure they were. But the most meaningful part of this excursion was the bond that Kate and I created. Only God could mend a heart like mine and bring two souls together to work with each other to help other people, like He did for us during that time.

In the following weeks, we planned to meet for lunches, and at them, we had beautiful conversations, filled with honesty, understanding, and an agreement to become friends, which is exactly what we did. To this day, we sometimes sit next to each other on Sunday mornings, and sometimes we make it to their annual Halloween party for the kids. Her smile no longer fills me with rage, but rather with gratitude. I'm so thankful for our bond.

Another beautiful friendship that the storm brought into my life was with Sarah. I don't have a clue as to the first time I met her, but a couple of weeks after the storm, she sent me a text that she was thinking about me and praying for us.

At first, I thought she was a different Sarah, but then I realized after some more messages that I didn't remember meeting her, but she went to my church. God definitely placed her in my life with purpose, because we became fast friends who needed each other to get through some really tough times.

Sarah was amazing. She and I grew close almost instantly, and we texted and hung out regularly. She was great at making lists, and although I usually was, my brain was always so discombobulated that I had difficulty sorting through my thoughts. She helped us move into our rental home from the cabin, gave me clothes from her closet so I could dress up for girls' date nights, and let me go through her jewelry to pick out pieces that I loved and kept.

She let me take soaps home from under her sink, invited Kory and me to stay the night when we needed a break and time away, and she invited us to the lake to spend hours in the sun. She and her husband even taught us how to wakesurf; they spent hours graciously teaching us how to glide the waves created by their boat. We had a blast.

Her friendship was exactly what I needed to break away from the everyday stress of putting our lives back together.

Her kindness was definitely a learned trait, because her family started to take us in, too. We spent Thanksgiving with them, went over for dinners, and even had a late-night bonfire together. Sarah and I bonded over marriage difficulties, and although hers didn't last, our friendship helped us both grow infinitely closer to God.

Throughout the whole time we both spent recovering together, me from the tornado and her through her divorce, even though we were very different, we learned to understand and respect each other in a way that only God can facilitate. The best part of our friendship is she moved onto Tornado Alley and lives just down the street from us. I thank God for her all the time.

CHAPTER 26

Marriage

Mark 10-9: "Therefore what God has joined together, let no man separate."

Marriage is a beautiful representation of love here on Earth, the way that Jesus loves the church. Because of its beauty and loveliness, evil will try to attack it from every angle. Stand together and hold firm in your love together. Marriage can endure all tests with God's support.

As I write this book, Kory and I have been married for eight years. Normally, I would say "eight wonderful years" or "eight loving years," but that wouldn't be the entire truth. Yes, they've been wonderful and loving for much of it, but we've been through some really tough times, too.

I'm sure you've heard people say that if you can build a house together, you'll stay married forever. This large undertaking is a "make or break" situation, due to the stress, the multitude of decisions that must be made, and the financial requirements, all of which always intensify relationships.

Well, they're right. Building a house together is hard. Building a house while one goes to school and you get two German Shepherd puppies is even harder. Let's get the in-laws involved, to help make decisions and work with you, and man, we were asking for it. Somehow, throughout the whole process, I only have wonderful memories. And guess what? We made it through, still married at the end, and before we even turned thirty!

Now, destroy that house and try to destroy the people inside of it. What really happened was we were drawn even closer together. When you lose everything but each other, your bond becomes even more strengthened. And trust me, we would need it, with everything we would have to face.

When we were displaced from our house to a hotel to a cabin, to the rental, and eventually back home again, our lives were constantly being uprooted. It felt as if we could never truly settle down and expect consistency. Living with the expectation of moving again so soon makes it difficult to want to make your situation livable, when you know it will only be for the short term, especially when the next step is unknown. What I mean by that is, what's the point of unpacking, putting things away, creating a schedule and routine with meal planning, or having a morning routine when you expect it all to change right away, anyway?

When this happens, you create an unstable environment in your home, and when the home isn't stable, nothing else in your life can be stabilized, either. After so much of this, it created a slowly-driven wedge between Kory and me.

When the pandemic was added to the mix, things got even worse. They weren't worse in the way you might expect, though. They were worse because now Kory was faced with more death, destruction, and dying every day, thirteen hours straight. Because of the heaviness of it all, he didn't want to talk about it when he came home, which led to me not knowing what he was experiencing each day at work or how greatly it really did affect him.

He carried that burden on his own. It was one he shared only with his coworkers, and soon, that bond began to grow greater than our marriage. We went through some really, really tough months involving marriage counseling and reprioritizing our relationship, because, to be honest, it had fallen to the wayside.

I couldn't relate to Kory or try to understand and support him, because he wouldn't let me in. Because I couldn't be the support he needed, he found it elsewhere with coworkers and people he didn't have to explain things to. They had been experiencing the heartbreak of watching people die alone, unable even to call loved ones due to the noise of the breathing machines they were on, which prevented the sick from communicating with anyone else.

It was so tragic and sad to hear that my husband had to hold the hands of the dying, but then would get pulled away to help stabilize another patient as their lungs began failing them, too. For over twelve hours a day, he experienced this repetitive tragedy, and then he came home to a wife who expected attention from him on top of everything else he'd experienced. It became too much, and at one point, it almost broke us.

The only explanation I have as to why we are married still to this day is through God's grace. At one point, I could have decided to become enraged and demanding and then left the house. It would have been the easiest choice, to just walk away from this hard situation. I had plenty of friends I could run to and parents in another state to support me. We didn't have a new house yet, so why go through the stress of rebuilding, if I couldn't and didn't want to connect with this person to whom I'd pledged my heart? We were different people than we had been when we got married, so it was perfectly understandable to just leave.

Except that it wasn't the easiest choice, not in the long run. That night, the night of all nights, when things had hit their absolute limit, I prayed a prayer to God and just asked Him to lead my heart.

Through the tears, the heart-wrenching sobs, and the hurtful words we had both said and heard that night, we came together, on the kitchen floor, and I prayed over us. It wasn't easy to put away my pride or feelings of righteousness. It wasn't easy to decide to stay together and work through the hard stuff. But let me tell you something, working through the hard stuff that night made it so we are now the strongest we have ever been.

Did you know, when you break a bone, your body works to recalcify it and make it stronger than before? Your body is amazing in the way it learns to grow and improve; this is one way it does so. Well, your resilience and commitment are built the same way. Experience something hard, work through it instead of walking away from it, learn from it, and grow through it. When you do that with another person, the bond becomes nearly unbreakable. When you add God into the equation, you become truly unbreakable.

Ecclesiastes 4:12 never rang more true to me than it did that year: Though one may be overpowered, two can defend themselves, but a cord of three strands is not quickly broken."

After that experience, building another house was a piece of cake. Our priorities had straightened out, our willingness to compromise had increased, and we really and truly wanted the other person in the relationship to be happy. Kory wanted me to have the closet of my dreams, so we prioritized it instead of fighting over the necessity of it. Kory wanted a man cave and place to store his whiskey and cigars, and after being very clear that there would be no cigar smoking in the house, I acquiesced, as well.

When the time came for us to move in, the house represented so much to us. Not only was it a new beginning on the same street, it was a new beginning for our marriage, a place to love each other and maybe a family. A place to welcome others and create bonds with new and old friends.

More than anything, it represented so much hope. Our first night in that house was an absolute blessing. It just needed to be the right timing, because two weeks later, we got that wish we had been dreaming of for three years.

We were pregnant.

CHAPTER 27

The Parent I Am

Isaiah 40:31: "Those who hope in the Lord will renew their strength. They will soar on wings like eagles; they will run and not grow weary, they will walk and not be faint."

God led me to my heart's desire of becoming a mother, after hoping and praying for so long. He gave me the strength and courage I needed to carry on, waiting for His timing to be perfect.

My longer-than-hoped-for journey to motherhood is not uncommon. Many women and families who are ready to grow can relate to my story, but most of us don't talk about that struggle. We don't talk about the disappointment we face each month, with every negative test, thinking, "Well, this one was wrong" or "I tested too early," and there is still a chance.

Every story is just as heart-wrenching and touching as the next for those people who yearn to know the plan for their lives and future families. Not all of them have found their happy endings yet, either, and my heart goes out to them. I know people say this all the time, but for us, it happened when we finally let our guard down and least expected it. When we let go and let God, it was within His plan.

The day we found out we were pregnant, it was by happenstance. I was getting ready for yoga early one morning. Kory lay snoozing in bed. I wondered how long it had been since I'd had my cycle. Since I kept a store of a hundred cheap pregnancy tests lying around, I thought I'd might as well test, to ease my mind and allow me to relax during the mindful meditation I was about to experience, and so my brain would not be going non-stop in the background, just wondering...

Y'all, there was absolutely zero expectation of a positive test, but it popped up in less than ten seconds. I couldn't believe my eyes. Heck, I could hardly see through the tears that were streaming down my face. I called out to Kory in what probably sounded like a desperate cry for help. I'm sure he thought something was terribly wrong.

He jolted up in bed as I entered the room with tears actively streaming down my face. Frantic and still half asleep, he asked, "What's wrong?!"

I don't remember if I blurted it out or merely showed him the test, but it took him a couple of seconds for the sleep to completely leave him so he could process what I had told him. His embrace around my waist was one of joy, love, and complete gratitude. We both held each other and let the news really sink in. I was of course filled with adrenaline and energy, but I decided I still wanted to go to yoga, because now I really had a reason to stay in shape and stretch my body.

It was as if a light switch had been turned on. I was sure that everyone would immediately know what was growing inside my belly just by looking at me. I felt purpose and hope and, honestly, a lot of fear, because what the heck had I gotten myself into?!

I frequently look back at my journey getting to that point and think about how different a parent I'd be, if I'd had sweet Beau before I was truly ready. I think about how much patience I wouldn't have had, how much anger I held in my heart, and how many things I wouldn't have known, in order to raise a child the way God wanted me to.

I think about the lack of involvement in my church he would have missed out on. The friends he wouldn't have, because my friends wouldn't have had their kids yet. I think of so many things that wouldn't have been able to align, if I'd had my darling at any other time in my life, even if we had managed to survive the storm that so many didn't.

After the storm, my priorities shifted. I found my purpose, and for the first time, I felt at peace and aligned with what God had placed on my heart. Because I was aligned in my heart, my actions changed, and my heart grew. My mindset was now focused on patience, forgiveness, and serving others.

This was also a period of significant growth, with prioritizing friendships, activities, and setting boundaries in order to make sure I had time for things that really mattered. Because I had different priorities, I had time for my son, instead of trying to fit him into our busy life.

How would I have known to do all of that if God hadn't taught me and I hadn't been open to learning it?

CHAPTER 28

Now

Jeremiah 29:11: "For I know the plans I have for you," declares the Lord. "Plans to prosper you and not to harm you, plans to give you hope and a future."

You are exactly where you are supposed to be. Your path is unique to who you are. We all go through different seasons, and that looks a little different to each of us. Sometimes we get off the path God put us on, but He always helps us find our way back.

If God had let me choose my path and the timing of my life, things would look a lot different from what they are like now. For one, if it was up to me, we would have had kids a lot sooner. To be honest, we would likely all have met the same fate as our friends who used to live down the street. The mom, dad, and one-year-old-son all perished together that night, and it's still a hard pill to swallow.

I also would not have waited so long to go to graduate school and figure my life out. If that had happened, I never would have been in school at the right time to meet my husband. I could sit here and play the "what if" game all day, but my point is, we would mess a lot of things up if the timing was up to us.

Many people could look at my situation and wonder how does one suffer so much yet come out so full of hope? Let me just tell you, it didn't happen overnight, and I wasn't always full of hope. It was through God's timing in my life and having a vulnerable heart that allowed me to slowly start to trust Him.

I went through many difficulties with each struggle I faced. The ultimate turning point for me, where I finally gave up control, happened the night I lost it all. Ironically, that's where my new beginning started. When you think of "new beginnings," I personally picture happy moments and a rebirth or days filled with sunshine and hope, but that obviously isn't how mine started. Rather, it was one that began with destruction; complete obliteration of a life and the things that made up that life, in order to make room for the new.

You see, when I lost everything, I was forced to rely on God for my strength, my provisions, and even for hope, because at one point, I truly had none. Through each little miracle, each little story, and each time God showed up, He rebuilt my faith and my life. He gave me hope that, if I continued to trust Him, He would continue to provide for me.

Now, this isn't to say that, after I started trusting God, the road was always easy, because that is not the case. My life involved a series of lessons, reflections, and self-growth that continue to challenge me to this very day. Something I learned from a few very mature people in my life is that growth is uncomfortable. If you feel unsettled, uneasy, or maybe like you don't belong where you are, it's probably because big changes are about to happen and God is preparing your heart.

I used to fear this feeling. It would add fuel to my anxiety, since I dreaded change or anticipated something negative was about to happen. It would fester inside my heart, making things ten-times worse than my original uneasy feeling. After the storm, my perspective began to change and grow. Now I can recognize the upcoming change and welcome it, because I know that God is working on my heart and in my life for the better.

Because I have begun to welcome the change, I have begun to allow hope to overtake my heart. When I know that God is working in my life in ways I cannot even imagine, it excites me, and I can hope for a future that is greater than the reality I'm living in now.

Now, I live in a beautiful house that still isn't fully decorated and still doesn't have pictures hanging in every room. I have an adorable son who is more stubborn than Kory and me put together and who has a brother on the way. I'm still terrified and excited when I think of all the blessings I have, everything it took to get to where I am now, and what is yet to come. This isn't something I could have learned any other way, except by living through my own experiences and learning in my own timing.

Someone could have told me the way they learned to have hope and trust in God, but it wouldn't have meant as much to me as my own story does. My hope is that I can help you to open your eyes to the lessons, disguised as struggles, that you face every day and see the purpose that each event has in our lives.

I hope you can notice the little events that happen in your life and recognize them as miracles, not just coincidences. Each set of shoes provided to you in unimaginable circumstances wasn't just happenstance; it was purposeful, and God thought of you when He did it.

Each red poppy flower or blue egg that appears in your life is a beautiful sign that God is working in your life and has your best interests at heart, giving you small little gifts as He molds you into the best version of yourself.

Writing my book hasn't been easy, but it's been full of purpose. I hope I can impact as many people as possible by sharing my trials and struggles but still maintain my hope and faith throughout. The last chapter has been the hardest, because I was so worried that I wouldn't summarize the experiences correctly or say the right thing or would leave something out. Finishing such a huge project has a sense of finality to it, making it real. I am putting my story out there for anyone to read and to judge, or to love or to hate, and that's scary.

I decided to sit and write out the final chapters of my story in my local bookshop, which has agreed to carry my book on their shelves, as well. While writing the final sentences, I couldn't help but smile as I listened to the chatter of the two young women tending the bookshelves. My heart was filled with joy as I began to imagine my book on the shelf that is dedicated to other local authors. My story is one of many, but I hope it's been as inspirational and full of hope for you to read as it's been for me to write.

TESTIMONIALS

From a Loved One's Lens

Kat is one of my oldest friends and is the most steadfast person I've met. She is as honest, caring, and loyal as my German Shepherds. Her support throughout the years has meant the world to me. Even though we haven't lived in the same state and sometimes not even the same country, since graduating from college, we have stayed close, always visiting each other and being there for the big events.

This time was no different. She came to be with me after the storm, to celebrate my birthday. She was there to listen to my book as I wrote it. She was the first person I called, when I found out I was pregnant again, even though she lived in Germany and was seven hours ahead of Tennessee.

Hearing her perspective on the morning after the storm broke my heart, because it's a different kind of hurt when your friends are hurting, even if it's for you.

* * *

"Have you heard from Lauren?"

Living in a different time zone, I grew accustomed to waking up behind on group texts, but this was different. Before I had even wiped the sleep from my eyes that morning, at least fifteen people had asked me the same question.

"Have you heard from Lauren?"

I talked to Lauren almost every day in one form or another. Many times, I woke up to messages from Lauren or at least in our group text with Hannah and Ashley. They both sent me a text with the same message, the same message I read over and over, trying to remove myself from the haze of last night's sleep.

"Have you heard from Lauren?"

I opened the search bar on my phone and typed Cookeville, Tennessee and selected "news." The only phrases I remember reading were catastrophic tornado and casualty count. *Where was Lauren?*

I called and texted anyone who might know anything, including everyone who had messaged me. Maybe news came through while I was still sleeping, and I hadn't been updated yet. So far, no one had heard anything. For the first time in a long time, I was worried about Lauren.

I met Lauren when we were eighteen years old. As the self-proclaimed mother hen of our group, I worried about everyone, at any time, for any reason. But not Lauren, not anymore.

Lauren had Kory and Cookeville; I didn't need to worry about Lauren. She'd found this man who was her perfect partner in every way. When I met Kory, I worried less. She'd found this place and community that fit her so beautifully. Every time I visited, I worried less.

Kory and Cookeville took my favorite parts of my best friend and made them better. She was bold, fearless, and self-assured. With her, everyone was invited, but more importantly, everyone was welcome. I was able to witness how Lauren poured herself into her community and her community poured back into her. It was beautiful and inspirational. However, right now, in this moment, I stopped being worried and was just terrified.

I can't remember the order of things, but at some point during that morning, I heard from Caitlyn, her sister. I could breathe again, knowing Lauren and Kory were alive and seemed to be physically unharmed. When I asked her what they needed, the answer was simple. They needed everything. We got to work.

Caitlyn, Hannah, Ashley, and I discussed who would send what. As we consumed the media coverage, the lists would change. As we watched our friend and her neighbors dig through the rubble of their lives, we realized the running shoes we'd agreed on wouldn't cut it. Add boots to the list. We knew it was cold, but now it was raining. Weather report said rain all week, so we needed to send better jackets or at least waterproof ones. And so it went, until Lauren and Kory told us they had enough for now.

About a week later, Lauren scheduled a call with Ashley, Hannah, and me, so she could tell us her story. We all had to be present, because she only wanted to tell us once. She also requested that we don't ask questions and not bring it up again until she was ready to revisit it. We all agreed, muted our phones, and listened to the most terrifying and somehow miraculous story I have ever heard. She told us what she could remember at that time, and I know there are many things I will hear for the first time reading this book.

For me, I have never stopped thinking about her finding shoes that night. I know beyond all reason and doubt that, if we ask God, He will give us shoes. And trust that, if we are steadfast in our faith and walk with Him, He will give us shoes twice.

* * *

My sister Caitlyn and I were never super-close growing up, mostly due to our separation in age and in school, but our venture into adulthood and the distance between us has brought us closer through the years. Her help with my book was a huge turning point, in my eyes, and has really strengthened our bond. I'm so grateful to have her in my life. She's talented, beautiful, and one of the strongest women I know.

To hear her have to experience the potential loss of family twice during a natural disaster was really hard to read and discuss, but I'm so grateful for her vulnerability and contribution to this book and my life. She has designed the cover, helped me with my website, and really taken the reins of helping me achieve my goals by using digital media. I love her so much, and this is just another beautiful example of God's intervention in my life to bring the right people closer to my heart.

* * *

My family is, unfortunately, familiar with traumatic natural disasters. Being a family member who lives a fair distance away, I know, when disaster strikes those you love, it is its own special hell. I've been that person twice.

In the aftermath of the 2018 Hurricane Michael that devastated our hometown of Panama City, Florida, Lauren and I weren't sure if our parents were alive for nearly twenty-four hours. Nearly every cell tower was down. We knew it was really bad, people had died, houses were destroyed, but we couldn't get ahold of them.

We only discovered they were probably okay when a friend of a friend of a friend on Facebook happened to post a photo of our parents' house from a distance, and someone tagged them in the comments. There were rugs, bath mats, and towels hanging from the front porch railing. Our parents are known to be on top of things, but they could only do that if they were alive, right?

Luckily, I got a phone call from them only a few hours later. The house was damaged, but they were fine. Such a relief.

In 2020, getting the phone call from Lauren was a little different. I don't remember exactly how soon after everything happened that she called me. All I remember is I got the call and was informed that, "There was a tornado. We're alive. The entire house is gone, but we're okay."

That's shocking news to receive in the middle of a work day. The danger came, wreaked havoc, and then was gone. Plus, Lauren's matter-of-fact delivery of this devastating information threw me. She seemed fine. Too fine. She must be in shock.

The first thing that went into my head was, "Do you have underwear?"

"I have... nothing."

"Okay, what kind do you like?"

Reacting to her stark admission of loss, I made an effort to fulfill her immediate needs, beginning with the simplest of necessities: underwear. Her resilience and calm demeanor in the face of such a disaster struck me even in that moment. Following the call, I reached out to our mom, to plan further support for Lauren, still in awe of the tremendous strength my sister was demonstrating.

You see, I'm pretty good in a crisis. When family members were concerned about Mom and Dad after the hurricane, I made it my job to handle communication, to call everyone, let them know what we knew and that they were all right.

It's tough, when you want to help people and you live so far away, so all you've got is your ability to help manage the onslaught of people who want to help and mean well, but it can get overwhelming. My sister especially struggles with that. When too many people come to her with questions or offers of help or even just kind words, it's too much. She tends to want to hide away from it all, even when it's kind and intended to be helpful.

Growing up, she was always looking out for me, as the older sister—even when she was being especially bossy. She took me to hang out with her friends and included me even when she didn't want to. She bought me food in college or took me out when she knew I was low on money. She drove me from school to gymnastics practice to home and more. She took care of me.

But somehow over the years, handling the storm of emotions became my role. Watching my sister go through these harrowing experiences, I saw her resilience and strength shine. From afar, I did my best to support her, taking charge of the emotional overflow, so she could focus on rebuilding her life and even processing what she just experienced. The hurricane in Panama City taught us both the importance of leaning on each other in times of need.

Lauren, grappling with the immediate aftermath of a life-altering event, deserved to be spared the stress of dealing with everyone else's emotions. I recognized her need for space and took it upon myself to coordinate with her friends, ensuring that their kind intentions translated into practical help. The reality of her situation became clearer with each conversation—how she would appreciate the practicality of jeans and could do without well-meant but less useful items.

To supplement the help from her insurance and community, Mom and I created a fundraising website for Lauren and Kory. Having lost literally everything, there was no such thing as too much help for them. As the donations flowed in, I saw how Lauren's story touched so many people. This recovery was going to take a village, and I was blown away by the outpouring of support. I cried when my coworkers gladly donated. It meant the world.

Looking back on the whole event, I'm confused by how logical and dry it all felt in those moments. I'm such an emotional person, yet when this happened to my sister, I somehow turned into an action-driven robot. She and Kory almost died. People on her street died. Children died. People lost everything. And I still struggle to feel the weight of it all.

Reading my sister's story has helped me see it through her eyes and feel those heavy feelings my body had shut out. We've since talked about it on the phone. I've listened to her rendition of it. The way the tornado sounded. The way it felt like it was happening in slow motion. How she had an out-of-body experience. Like she was watching a war scene in a movie.

Through reading her words here, I'm able to truly understand the enormity of the event from her perspective. It's with immense gratitude that I think of their survival—Lauren, Kory, and even my beloved fur-nieces. In the aftermath, I've witnessed the testing of Lauren and Kory's relationship, their struggles only serving to solidify their bond, making it stronger than ever before. I'm thankful my sister hadn't had a child yet, because I'm not sure I'm strong enough to handle the loss of a niece or nephew. The story of what her neighbors lost breaks my heart every time I think about it.

I remember thinking they could finally move away and get a fresh start. Maybe move closer to me or our parents. Maybe move somewhere closer to the coast. But somehow, Lauren and Kory's love for their neighbors and their community only grew. The wind tried to rip up their roots, and they responded by digging in deeper.

I've seen my sister transform through this traumatic event, and it's nothing short of extraordinary. She didn't just survive a tornado;

she rose above it, each hurdle shaping her into an even more resilient and courageous woman. She's been able to find the smallest silver linings, even laugh at the absurdity of it all, and that in itself is a testament to her strength.

Lauren has used this experience not as an anchor holding her back, but as a force propelling her forward. Her love with Kory, too, has become stronger, weathering this literal storm together. I cherish them both and can't help but feel awed by their resilience. This experience has changed them, but undeniably for the better.

My family is now blessed with their son, Beau, and the little boy they're expecting later this year. Their future holds nothing but growth and promise, and I can't wait to see where life takes them next. Through it all, I remain incredibly proud to call this extraordinary woman my sister.

* * *

For more information about Lauren's story and additional support for anyone suffering a tragedy, visit www.drlaurenfarmer.com.

ACKNOWLEDGMENTS

When I think of people who have influenced my life, and specifically those who have played a role in my story and contributed to my book, the list is quite literally endless. A large fear of mine is leaving someone out or making someone feel like their contribution went unnoticed, when, in actuality, my brain just doesn't have the ability to recall the thousands of miracles I've experienced and witnessed. Well, here goes my attempt.

First and foremost, I want to recognize my parents, John and Shelli. Without their upbringing and teaching me I really could do anything I put my heart to, I wouldn't be doing all these things that, at some point, I decided I needed to be doing. I remember the first time I went to buy a car as an adult. When I told my dad my plans, concerned about all the "what-ifs," including what if I ever lost my job, I remember him telling me, "Lauren, I'm not worried about you, because you always find a way." That has really stuck with me and encouraged me to be resilient. It's also made me confident that, if he believed in me, so should I. My mother raised my sister Caitlyn and me to be independent self-thinkers, but she also taught us the grace that goes with being a good wife and mother, and in embracing the feminine charm that she so graciously displays.

I'm forever grateful to my sister, Caitlyn, who not only brought my dreams to life by designing this cover, but who has been my second rock, next to my husband, Kory, through this book's editing and creating process. We've grown so close this year, and I'm forever grateful for how this process has done that. You were right, SJ, the process of writing a book changes lives and relationships. I'm also grateful to her for helping to fundraise from across the country and for being everyone's point of contact, so no one disturbed me as I tried to piece my life back together.

An enormous thank you goes out to my in-laws, both sets! Cindy and Kip and Becky and Paul—all of you have played very different and important roles during the past decade of my life. But the most important part is you raised the perfect husband for me. You created him into a man who is hard-working, serving, and would have given his life for mine that night. Thank you for the help after the tornado and as we put our lives back together. I'm so glad I have three amazing families to rely on.

Thank you so much to Kyle and Ashley, who helped set up fundraising for us, despite having their own home affected by the tornados. We would not have our first home and, honestly, parts of our second without Kyle's amazing handiwork and willingness to lead us to smart contracting decisions. Thank you for all the hours you've spent helping us in so many ways. Thank you to Ashley for buying my first outfit after that storm and for helping me to feel like myself again.

To Kat and Hannah, thank you so much for helping Caitlyn after the storm to get things organized and over to me. I don't have clear memory of this time, but I know what an instrumental role you played in getting me shoes, a raincoat, socks, underwear, and cute outfits, plus helping with my fundraiser. Your support continues to bring tears to my eyes every time I think about it.

To my Collegeside church family. A few days after the storm, you hosted a prayer night for everyone to come together and pray for the community and for those lost, and to pray for Hensley Drive and all the families on that street. This was the first sign of your support. I remember feeling so loved and grateful that night. All I owned, I carried on my back in my black backpack, and that's all I needed at that time. In the weeks and months to follow, you lent financial support to my family, helped get lost items returned to us, and gave me hope for the future. You set up a base camp and allowed me to come and go as I needed.

My heartfelt gratitude to the wonderful group of women from church. I can't even tell you how grateful I am to you for helping us clean up our lot, but also for loving Kory and me through this terrible time. You were there to pick up my ripped wardrobe off the dirty, muddy floor and take it to your home, shake out as much glass as you could, and then place load after load into your own washing machine. You then folded each piece like it was the most delicate item in someone's closet and gave it all back to me, so I could decide what to keep and what to toss. Your gentleness has been such an inspiration in my growth to becoming a Godly woman.

To Kara and Beau, thank you for giving me a laptop, running point at church, and just being a beacon of light. You helped me watch baby Beau after he was born and opened your family and home to us. I just love giving you hugs at church!

To Rachel, thank you for allowing Kory and the girls and me access to your beautiful home during our transition. We created a bond that both of us needed so badly, and I'm forever grateful to you for cleaning your home and allowing me to feel like I had a place of my own again.

To Megan and Ben, thank you so much for giving us access to your beautiful cabin for an entire month and for hosting us in your basement on the nights when the weather got to be too much. We so appreciated your sharing your land with us.

To Brittney and Jon, thank you for letting us stay in your basement when we needed to feel extra-safe. Thank you for your support and love and for helping us install the best windows around in our new home! Your guidance and support are inspirational.

To the Cookeville Police Department and the officers who allowed me to help them distribute the semitrucks of supplies, thank you. You easily could have turned me away and said no, or told me, because of covid, I couldn't be there. Instead, you permitted my creativity to shine and allowed me to connect you to the community. You helped me to feel needed, like my life still mattered after losing everything.

Also, to all of the Putnam County Sheriff's officers who helped keep our property and belongings safe by setting up patrols and dispersing the onlookers from treating us like a zoo, thank you. I'm so thankful that you even showed up with four officers at 2 a.m. and didn't try to arrest my husband, who was sleeping there to protect our newly delivered windows. Thanks for protecting us and our things from people who lack that same respect. Also, thanks for not shooting my husband when he who rolled out of his hammock and onto our German Shepherd, who didn't turn out to be a great guard dog that night.

To the entire Cookeville community, who helped work the community center and handle returned items, thank you for taking your time to give me back a piece of my former life. Even the shredded pictures, torn belongings, and damaged goods still meant something to me. Your care of them meant the world to me, too. Thank you to anyone who turned in pictures found in your yard or at your business.

To Jefferson Avenue Church of Christ, thank you for helping us with our furniture and giving us supplies during our time in need. There are so many other churches that also gave us help, though I cannot remember them all individually. But each one greatly impacted us and made us feel so much love from God and His people.

To Brittney and Jared, thank you so much for providing us shelter that night after the storm. Thank you for giving me another great reason to move back into this neighborhood, and thank you for being great neighbors and friends. We love doing life together with y'all!

To Julie and Eric, thank you for reaching out and being our friends and neighbors. It meant the world to me when you thought to bring me hairspray and a blow dryer from your salon, when I never thought to reacquire those important beauty products myself.

Thank you, Megan, for letting me use your house as a delivery point for sending all my packages for months. Thank you for giving me my beautiful dinner plate back, after I gave it to you years ago. Thank you for buying me makeup and being such a great friend to me during that rough time.

Amy and Darrell, thank you for providing shelter for so many that night. Thank you for being the neighborhood watch and always treating us like family. Our bond is so strong. I'm so grateful for y'all.

Macy and Matt, there aren't words to tell you what your friendship has meant to us. We went through something horrendous together, and our lunches and talks after the storm helped us heal so much. Thank you for half of the beautiful land that our new home sits on. I'm so grateful this is where our home is.

To our entire Hensley family, we will always be a neighborhood, no matter where we all live. Thank you to each person who played a crucial role in the rescue of one another. I'm so thankful for our Zoom calls during lockdown, our coffee meetups, and everyone's support through the process of my telling my version of what happened that night.

Thank you to the Red Silo Brewing Company for the first fundraiser we received, which was such a significant relief for us, as we didn't have wallets or other means at the time. We always felt like family there, and we love the family-friendly environment you've created.

Thank you to the Red Silo Runner's Club and all those who helped provide food for Xena and Shadow for a month, while we couldn't. As we focused on putting our lives back together, the enormous relief from stress that you gave us is indescribable

To Liz, thank you for your search for my wedding dress and for returning such a special item back to me. You are a friend for life!

To Cookeville K-9 and Friends, I can't even begin to say thank you enough. Your willingness to just take our girls in and not only love them, but then also to order them new dog beds, toys, and bones was so touching. Shannon, you will forever hold a special place in my heart.

To David and Johnson's Nursery, thank you for saving my plant babies and caring for them for an entire year, until they could find their home again. I have so much joy walking in my garden and seeing all the other survivors, and it's because of you!

Thank you to Tex, Mitzi, and Pappy's Place for the gift from fundraising at your establishment and then for thinking of us. What an honor.

Thank you to all of the volunteers who came in, locally and from all over the country, to help us recover. From those students who helped pick up trash on our lot to the people who brought in heavy-duty equipment to dig up the footers of our old house so we could start fresh, everyone's support has meant so much.

To the Cloyd family, thank you for supporting our local families with the generous donation from your church.

To Andy, Kory's dear friend, thank you for coming up as soon as you heard the news, driving for hours to come support us and help us heal.

To Stephanie, thank you for helping so much at church and letting me help you help other families. You connected so many people to things they needed.

To Sarah Beth and Hope, thank you for new friendships and the help you gave my family after the storm. You were the girlfriends God knew I needed.

To Thomas, for lending us a car and for always being at the right place at the right time, when we needed some extra help.

Thank you to Tennessee Tech University Archives and all those involved in helping return pictures and lost items to us. Thank you also to those who worked at the fairgrounds to distribute supplies and allow us to collect lost items.

Thank you to the Plenty Bookstore, for agreeing to carry my book and for supporting me through the journey of writing. I loved sitting in your cozy chairs to type out pieces of my story.

To Cookeville Regional Medical Center Foundation and all the nurses on 5 North, thank you for your support and for loving us through our recovery. Thank you for taking care of our neighbors and helping them heal.

Thank you to all the members of our Collegeside church family whom I wasn't able to name individually. You each have meant so much to me, and even if I don't remember your name, I promise I'm working on it. I'm so grateful for all the prayers and hugs. Even though I'm not a huge hugger, the support means so much.

To everyone who donated any amount to our fundraisers set up by friends and family, thank you. Thank you for taking from your own pot and giving to us in our greatest time of need. We were able to distribute some of that to others in need who did not have the resources or reach that we did. It was beautiful to see God's hand in ensuring so many people were helped due to your generosity.

To our USAA insurance agent, Will—you were so easy to work with and such a blessing to us. You handled everything in a way that we didn't have to stress about. So many of our neighbors and friends had to deal with the headache of other insurance agencies, but not us. You stuck with us for an entire year, and I'm so grateful for you.

To Matthew with the Jewelry Emporium, thank you for helping me restore the ring my husband bought me before the storm. Thank you for cleaning my surviving jewelry pieces and helping us find the perfect replacement diamond ring.

To that woman in the grocery store who bought my groceries the day I lost my credit card and didn't have enough cash on me to cover groceries. You didn't care that it was a silly mistake or that I was almost in tears, trying to decide what to put back. One look at my pregnant belly and the baby in the cart with me, and your Momma Bear instinct kicked in. You rescued me and my sanity that day.

To Kylee-girl. If you hadn't dragged me to another one of your events, with some crazy idea that "I had to be there," then this book would *not* be here. You encouraged me to step out of my comfort zone so many times, and I'm so grateful for that, because at that event, I met SJ, my publisher, and started on this crazy journey.

To SJ, obviously, this book wouldn't be here and wouldn't be of this caliber, if you hadn't pushed me to dig really deep and tell more than my story from that night. To include my story from childhood and how I've recovered. You helped bring out the best, and the worst parts, which really helped me to help people relate to my story and see God's hope.

To all the young women out there who have no idea what to do with their lives, who don't know how to love or be loved, and who don't know how they fit into God's plan yet—I see you. I *was* you. It will all work out, if you pray, trust God, and be a good person with a kind soul. Your story will turn out to be something big someday, too, with the potential to help so many other people.

ABOUT THE AUTHOR

Lauren Farmer is the wife to a wonderful husband and her perfect soulmate and mother to two energetic and wild little boys. But most of all, she's an imperfect Christian who tries to be the best version of herself, loved and created by God.

She has her bachelor's degree in business from the University of Florida and her doctorate in physical therapy, obtained from the University of St. Augustine in 2015. She has practiced in myriad clinical settings, including most recently on pediatrics, where she leads a team of therapists to enhance the lives of children in Middle Tennessee.

After surviving the sixth deadliest tornado in Tennessee's history, she found herself on a path of recovery and healing. On that journey, her eyes were opened to the many miracles God had placed in her life, leading her to each and every decision, including aligning her life to enable her to write this book.

www.ingramcontent.com/pod-product-compliance
Lightning Source LLC
Chambersburg PA
CBHW030006290326
41934CB00005B/244

9 781959 955023